Glenn!
You are the
best ♡

10/28/2?

A Fresh Perspective
creating a lifestyle business

Renate A. Moore

SPARK Publications
Charlotte, North Carolina

A Fresh Perspective: Creating a Lifestyle Business
Renate A. Moore

Designed, produced, and published by SPARK Publications
SPARKpublications.com
Charlotte, North Carolina

Developmental Editing by Sherré L. DeMao

Photos
Photoongraphy / New Africa / Shutterstock.com
Author photos and lemon bars by SnapHappy Photos
Photo illustrations by SPARK Publications.

Printed in the United States of America.

First Edition paperback, July 2023, ISBN: 978-1-953555-58-8
Library of Congress Control Number: 2023909827

To my husband and family,
who were the force behind the
amazing business and lifestyle I
created to be home with them.

For Daddy, whose wisdom and
love will forever be my guide.

Contents

When life gives you lemons,
make something sweet.

Introduction

Full disclosure: I am a self-taught businesswoman who developed my company by thinking outside the box and using some unconventional methods. I do not have an MBA or any experience working with top-ranking corporations. The way I built my company would never be taught in business schools nor be found in a textbook. However, these methods worked for me and have captured the interest of other women business owners who wanted to learn from someone like me.

If you are reading this right now, chances are you are like these women who were intrigued with my journey and wanted to learn how I did it. It is because of these women I decided to write this book for you. I realized I had wisdom to share that could save others time, money, frustration, heartache, and mistakes.

I spent endless hours figuring out how to get started and then another five years before I actually launched. Yes, you heard that right—five years! Everything felt like a struggle, from finding the information on how to start a business to understanding the business and legal language that makes policies difficult to understand. There were so many moving parts and requirements that were all new to me. Chances are you have felt this too if you have already started your journey as a business owner. After I finally started the business, I stepped into another world of challenges. One challenge after another after another, it seemed.

I don't want you to fight your way through like I did. As you turn the pages of this book, you will see that I tried many things, some of which worked, and some didn't. But through them all I gained great experiences and learned many lessons.

I wrote this book to share my real-world experiences and lessons on building a woman-owned business. I hope to clarify your business journey and help you see personal success sooner. This is for women like you who seek to have a lifestyle or small business and want to feel informed and encouraged.

Yes, life has a way of giving you lemons. I turned my lemons into Super Star Lemon Bars and a lifestyle business that allows me to love my life too. Your lemons could be what truly take your business to levels you never considered before. Good things do come from bad situations, but there are struggles and challenges that also come with them. Finding ways to bridge the gap from the concept of starting a small business to surviving and thriving in the world of women business ownership is what this book is about. It's about having a business you love as well as a life you love. One goal does not have to be sacrificed for the other.

I will tell you the truth about the perseverance I needed, the encounters I had, and the mistakes I made when starting my business. I got started in a new state where I did not know anyone, and business ownership was a whole new world to me. I worked in the corporate sectors prior to becoming an entrepreneur. Owning a business was never something

I envisioned or even dreamed of doing, but a new path led me there.

I had an idea about what I wanted to do, but I felt like a fish out of water. I knew I had to start somewhere and surround myself with people who had "been there and done that"— people who were further along in their journey. However, finding those people and opportunities were not as easy as I expected. I was new to town with an uprooted lifestyle where life seemed to spare me no lemons.

Let me save you time *and money*, dear reader, and help you learn from what I went through. Whether you are starting or growing your business, or looking to make a change in your personal life, my intention is to help you reach the highest levels of your creative potential and dig deep into the wisdom within you. Throughout this book, I will show you the steps I took to get started, breaking it down so not only do you feel you can do it, but you feel supported and affirmed. These recommended best practices provide a clear and concise guide to help you get started or take your business to its next level. I wish I had this information ten years ago when I was starting out, and that is why this book exists—to be that source of guidance to you.

Instead of wandering into the hot oven without mitts, now you will have a recipe to follow and the tools you need for success.

Double knot your apron!
Dose up your courage!
Put on those mitts!
And get ready to SIZZLE!

Recipe for Success

A Profitable
Lifestyle Business

A Sprinkle of Courage

A Zest of Faith

A Smear of Resilience

A Pinch of Focus

A Dollop of Planning

A Drizzle of Execution

A Palmful of Creativity

A Dash of Positivity

A Splash of Opportunities

Chapter One
Not My Cup of Tea

There's always a backstory, and here is mine. It all began in the year 2003 with an uprooted lifestyle. My family and I relocated from New York to North Carolina due to my husband's job. We sold our home, and I resigned from a job that I loved. With my background in real estate, Wall Street, and international education, I had always worked in the corporate world. It was rewarding and hard earned.

Now I was in a new place with no relatives, no friends, and no job. The city life I adored was replaced with farmland and unfriendly people, lack of social activities that I was used to, and the inability to go to places easily by train or walking. I missed the culture and food, the boutiques and styles of clothes. I missed civilization.

I was very sad, nervous, and worried. I had moved from a cosmopolitan city to a place that appeared unaccepting of outsiders. It felt as though people in this new area were not as receptive or welcoming to those who appeared to be from a particular country or certain part of the world, or those who had a different ethnicity or accent. These were some of my impressions when we first arrived, and yet I couldn't fully understand why.

Our realtor broke his promise to help me acquire a job and to introduce me to the community, and that made me angry because he did not keep his word. Looking back, I ask myself, "What was I thinking? Why the heck would I have trusted him to help me find a job?" Then I realized it was weakness. It was easier for me to trust someone who was not me—a person who I hoped would be my savior at that moment—because that is what I needed. However, that was just an illusion; I had to accept that I was putting my future into someone else's hands instead of my own.

After many disappointments seeking employment in this new town, being overlooked, and facing the challenges of being a minority woman of color, I had given up on the idea of having a career. I spent the following four years getting acclimated and trying to find friends, to fit in—and that became my lifestyle. Needless to say, I was not happy.

I believe we experience change for a reason and that change often comes in four phases: panic and pause, adapt, re-create, and embrace.

1 - Panic and Pause (Receive a Bushel of Lemons)

Here I was without my normal routine, surrounded by unfamiliar faces, and trying to find some positive outlook with this change. My four-year pause to get acclimated was a choice, yet it came with unwelcome consequences. My panic had set in, and I was in a state of true frustration with living here. Then one morning it happened. While I was standing at the bus stop with my eight-year-old daughter, surrounded by the neighborhood mom group who had no desire to get to know me despite my attempts, across the street stood an older woman with her granddaughter. She waved and warmly greeted me; after the children got on the bus, she came over and introduced herself and asked if I was new to the neighborhood.

I was relieved that I made contact with someone who acknowledged me and was interested in building a relationship. The conversation we had was warm and encouraging. This lady made me feel hopeful to continue living in this new place. I felt that my family and I finally found someone we could turn to for assistance if we needed it. This small action gave me hope. I was pausing—and that transformed my panic into hope.

2 - Adapt Ingredients (Adjust Your Recipe)

What came after that chance meeting was a welcoming conversation which grew into a friendship; and even though she was much older than me, it was better than having no friends. This was something I might not have pursued if I was still living in New York. But that is the reality of new experiences: you must be flexible and embrace opportunities that come your way.

I might not have considered a friendship because of the age difference. This person was in her seventies. I was in my thirties. The friends and colleagues I knew in New York were within my age group. We shared similar interests. Why would I spend time with someone much older than I with a different mindset? Our conversations were very different, yet what that revealed to me was a reminder that I adapt easily, and I am indeed accepting of everyone. That experience opened my mind to finding ways to be creative and seeking out new ways of doing things. It gave me confidence to improvise and practice skills I've never tested before. When faced with panic, it is easy to feel paralyzed and uncomfortable with the lemons you have been handed.

Your power lies in being open to adapting, even when you don't realize it or want to at that time.

3 - Re-create Your Recipe (Implement the New Recipe)

I changed my mindset to make it suitable for a new purpose, and shortly after, I realized that I had left the phase of panic behind, had adapted, and was now creating my new normal, which I came to recognize was a much-needed adjustment and a breath of fresh air from the New York lifestyle I thought I couldn't live without.

I applied a technique I'd learned from my father. He taught me the power of the brain and how habits work. To start a new habit, you need to not be mired in expectations. Instead of wasting energy on expectations, it is best to switch to an attitude of adjustment and experimentation. Who do I wish to become? What do I stand for? What results would I like to see? And so I chose to be present and to make the most of whatever was in front of me, seeing what transpired, and what felt right, and was sustainable.

4 - Embrace New Habits (Test the Recipe)

This phase happened when I accepted and understood the value of change. Like most of you, I found comfort in my old habits and hobbies and would avoid change, but I desired something different; that desire gave me courage to take some risks and to step away from what was comfortable but not serving me. This time, I fully embraced my present circumstances. I accepted my new hometown and decided not to lament over what I no longer had. Instead, I visualized the benefits that could come from this change and embraced my new beginning by putting a spin on the things that I enjoy. Since I love cooking and talking about healthy living, I could combine food and education into a unique business. I'd still be engaging in work except I would be creating a business on my terms while having more time for myself and my family.

Knowing these four stages of change helps us as human beings to overcome comfortable old habits and practices and to embrace the change we truly desire. After much contemplation and assessment of "then and now," I learned to see change as new experiences awaiting me; it was then easier for me to leave behind my old habits and to activate my no-going-back mindset.

In hindsight, I realize that I was desperate. I easily trusted people who crossed my path if I believed they were going to help me make connections and provide the services I needed, but too often I was left with disappointment. When you are desperate, you make mistakes in trusting people who will deceive or mislead you. You trust them because it feels much easier than trusting yourself to do the hard work. That was why I believed that realtor and many others.

Focusing on what I could control allowed me to leave behind the desperation and disappointments, opening my mind to new possibilities.

Recipe for Success:

Better Way to
Approach Uncertainty

Don't believe everything you think is the right fit.

Be open to a totally different possibility.

Accept that you cannot control all that transpires,
but you can control what is in your power.

Trust in yourself and believe things will work out,
even if it's not the way *you* expect.

I believe we experience change
for a reason
and that change often comes in
four phases:
panic and pause, adapt, re-create,
and embrace.

Chapter Two
Creative Juices Flowing

My husband, Keith, has always been my sounding board and beloved confidant, so he knew I did not like where we had moved to and that I was very unhappy. I was angry that I had no purpose (or so it felt). Keith always found ways to help me see possibilities. While I was telling him again how much I disliked being here and that I *hated* it, he reminded me that I've always wanted to write children's books. Instead of focusing on finding a job, he suggested that I use the time to pursue my writing interest.

At first, I was adamant about not wanting to do that because all I could think about was not having the New York lifestyle and salary that I was accustomed to. But that day of encouragement from Keith made me think a little differently. I decided to pursue my writing, something I had set aside for a later time in life. Perhaps the time was now after all.

As fate would have it, I stumbled upon a magazine in a doctor's office with information for a writing school where I was accepted upon my application. During that process, I wrote several manuscripts which led to becoming a published children's book author

The idea for the business originated when I had an "aha" moment as I was writing my first children's book, *A Frog in Grandma's Cup.* What if I combined my food knowledge and expertise, along with my corporate skills, to create a job for myself? I saw the need for literacy and better-quality foods and felt strongly about providing something with originality that would make a difference in our community.

I am a caring person and whenever I see there's room for improvement, I look for solutions. My new hometown was lacking in fresh-baked goods. My family and I recognized that these products were made with low-grade ingredients, and I felt I could be an advocate for change through my own example.

Prior to this epiphany, one of my retirement wishes was to have a small quaint café and bookstore. As I contemplated the thought, I started the conversation with Keith one evening while we were out having coffee at a local shop. I shared my vision of having a café where I would serve a healthier option of baked goods and shelve children's books for families to enjoy with their children. I told him I had this idea: What if I created an online business that I can consider my café? I will sell my pastries and children's books so customers can shop virtually. Keith was supportive and encouraged me to go for it. Of course, I had no idea what it would take or how to get started, but I positioned myself in places to meet people and start the conversation.

Health and wellness are a lifestyle to me that began with learning about food and cooking at an early age in my mother's kitchen in British Guiana (now Guyana) in South America. My working mom loved to cook and wanted to pass that love on to my brother and me, so she would have us help as sous-chefs in the evenings as she prepared meals. My dad, a Charles Atlas bodybuilder graduate, introduced us to athletics and fitness and the benefits of nourishment for the mind and body.

Once when my mom was in the hospital, my dad, brother, and I had to pitch in to prepare meals. We did not have fast food there.

Everything was prepared from scratch. This meant going to the market; buying fresh fish, meat, and vegetables; and harvesting additional vegetables from our garden.

As I reflected on my upbringing, I realized I was about to pursue an idea that I was uniquely prepared to offer. In chapter 16, I share how the secret ingredient is you. I want you to ponder on this a little bit as you continue to read this book, because you truly are the secret ingredient—once you begin to realize it.

I also had to get my head into a place that would finally free me from the belief that I needed to be working for someone else in order to have the lifestyle I so missed. I did a deep reflection on what being free of the corporate world and being my own boss could help me realize.

Once I was no longer in a corporate workplace setting, I would have the luxury of setting my work hours, which would allow me flexibility to schedule my day. I wouldn't have to be at my desk from 9 a.m. to 5 p.m. I would decide when I start and when I end. In my previous careers, the company set my work hours. Now I would set my own boundaries for work.

I also thought about the fact that when you work for someone else, your ideas may not get the attention they deserve, whether you're working in corporate America or for someone else. I recognized that if I was my own boss, I could implement ideas or take calculated risks without needing a manager or boss's approval, unlike when I worked in corporate.

Being present when my children came home from school and being able to attend their athletic and school events without needing someone's authorization was also appealing and important to me. I am glad I made that choice because I was able to keep my children on the right path by being present while still fulfilling my desire for meaningful work.

I've always had a morning routine where I take a few minutes to reflect on where I am and what I have, as well as to sift the positive out of recent experiences. This habit helped me embrace the realization that I could choose for myself who and what I want to be associated with.

My mind was made up. I was going to go all in and do this idea of a business, without fully realizing or knowing what I was truly getting into. I was creatively excited and energized by what the possibilities could be. I was ready, or so I thought!

Recipe for Success:

Beauty of Being Your Own Boss

You set your own work hours
and control your schedule.

You implement ideas that come to
mind without needing approval.

You make your family a
priority while still having a career.

You choose which organizations
benefit from your time and expertise.

You choose who you want to work with and why.

Chapter Three
Preheating & Prepping

As I said in the introduction, it took me five years from the time I came up with the idea to actually launch my business. I needed that time to turn my own recipe for success into a thriving business because I was starting with a blank page—no ingredients or instructions. I knew I had to start somewhere. Once I figured out what my business was about, I spent the next five years working on the structure.

I began with what I was familiar with: the internet and research—lots and lots of research! I spent hours researching the requirements for starting a business in my industry. I knew I had to invest long hours, but I honestly did not realize how exhausting it could be. When my children went to sleep, I stayed up past midnight doing my research. The benefit of the internet is that there is a lot of valuable information out there; you just have to put in the time and effort to find it.

But the downside to the internet is that it can overwhelm you, sending you in many directions if you are not focused. Having so many options was leading to information overload. I'd gather so much information that I would become anxious and freeze, losing the ability to make the right decisions because I was now thinking that I must at least consider or even do them all.

I realized very quickly I needed to simplify the research I was doing based on a list of questions to effectively start my business.

Questions to Stir the Pot

I wrote out everything I needed to know and anything I thought I might need to do in order to make informed decisions.

The following list includes questions I wished I would have asked.

- What are the start-up essentials for launching a business?
- What are the requirements of starting a business in this state?
- How can one register and obtain a business license in the state? Is a license required in my county or city?
- What legal documents are required?
- What are some affordable and trusted legal firms?
- How do I build a website?
- What are some cost-effective website platforms with basic designs?
- How do I obtain a business phone number?
- Do I need a business address? Can a PO Box be used as a business address?
- How can I trademark the business logo and other business images?
- What are the steps to getting a logo designed?
- How much money should I have to start a business?
- What happens if the business fails?

Who's around the Kitchen Table Matters

Awareness of strengths and weaknesses is important. I have very little knowledge of business law, accounting, and financial planning. These three disciplines were key in helping me with any business forms and information that needed to be maintained, and they will be valuable to you too.

An attorney will guide you through properly setting up your business and understanding the legalese in contracts and agreements. An accountant will help avoid any problems with your taxes and the IRS. A financial planner will guide you through managing your money. And all three are going to help you set your business up for success.

Be sure to shop around and interview a few people and businesses before making your selection. I've had some unfavorable experiences with some of the people I had on my team, including my initial accountant, before I finally found the right advisory partners for my business's success. The experiences with those that didn't work out taught me how to improve the vetting process for these services.

Make sure you understand all the verbiage they are using. The professionals to hire are those who help you understand instead of making you feel like a fool for not knowing. Gather all of this information from your advisory team to put your plan in place, then make the decisions. Remember these are your decisions, first and foremost, because your name is on the line.

Since I've been through the process, I now know that you can get your feet off the starting block before the five-year mark. It took me five years to launch the business because I was in a place where I was figuring out things for myself. Many support systems did not work for me. Monies invested were lost, and I had to start all over again. When this book is completed in its entirety, you will understand two things:

(1) why it took me five years to get off the starting block, and (2) how you can get off the starting block sooner by knowing what I didn't know.

Recipe for Success:

Launching Your Business

Simplify your research by knowing what answers you need now to get started effectively.

Make an attorney, accountant, and financial planner a part of your advisory team.

Have all agreements in writing and read the fine print before signing a contract.

Understand what's required of your business by the IRS and other government agencies.

Chapter Four
Small Bites, Big Launch

O nce I found the information I was looking for, I went to work. I broke down the tasks into smaller pieces. I used money from my personal savings in order to avoid additional bills in our household expenses, so I implemented a method that I called *piecemealing the process*.

I considered piecemealing the process to be an unconventional method because, unlike many new entrepreneurs, I did not want a bank loan. I did not want to incur additional debt that would impact our family's finances. I was not working; therefore, there was no second income. My husband's career was the only income.

Applying this method and by using money from my retirement account saved us the burden of too much debt and hefty overhead expenses, while also staying focused on our children's educational costs. This would allow me to limit expenses and to avoid a monthly bill from taking out a business loan or accumulating large credit card debt with high interest rates and minimum payments.

To piecemeal the process required some planning as well as setting priorities. I made a list of the projects in order of priority and focused on moving from one to the next. I would then commit to one or two, depending on the costs. However, it was also important to decide what was most urgent or important and not letting the cost be the only deciding factor.

Here is how I segmented my initial list.

Urgent & Important to Business Starting	Important to Business Starting
• Legal business structure • Securing website domain • Business registration and business licenses • Setting up a business phone and internet service	• Graphic designer for logo • Developing website • Website maintenance • Marketing messaging and support

I prioritized the first items needed to start a business: the legal structure and setup. Then the next to be considered was the website domain related to the company name. And that's how I went down the list, focusing first on what was urgent and essential and then moving to what was important to have prior to launch, leaving the least important for the last step and continuously reprioritizing when items were checked off the list.

I started with a professional legal service to help me acquire all the business structure registration and licenses, as well as to handle all the required legal documents. Law is complicated and for each business industry there may be unique rules. I knew I would save myself wasted time and money by filing the right forms and stating correct information from the very beginning. If any issues arose, my lawyer would represent me.

After paying for those services, I moved on to the next item on the list. While I had one or two projects in process, I was gathering information for the next ones, preparing a budget, and seeking the resources to get them done.

I'm a planner and an organized person. Part of my self-reliant teachings growing up were learning how to manage finances and how to prepare to invest. Creating a budget was easy for me to do because it came from a skill I implemented. This is something I did right, but I have seen many business owners not pay attention to budgeting, and I want better for you. Too many business owners operate by the seat of their pants without a budget, thinking that a budget doesn't matter since they are just starting. I cannot emphasize enough the importance of budgeting and the headaches you will diminish by planning with a budget based on the priorities you set.

If you have technical or office skills, use them. For example, if you have experience in data processing and information technology, use those skills to build your website. Apply administrative skills to organize your files and bookkeeping skills to maintain your accounting records. This is just to get you off the ground without having to shell out a lot of money to hire assistants. I applied my corporate background skills and expertise to the administrative part of the work and used my husband's IT skills to build a basic website.

Long-term debt is not something I've ever been eager to have. To establish credit, we must have some debt, and for that reason, I only incur debt that won't affect our household. I did not want to be in a position where I had large amounts of debt but not enough net income to pay them back. I did not want investors because, again, I wanted to maintain control based on what I could afford and not have outside pressures or have liens on personal assets.

This step-by-step process helped me move forward, a little slower perhaps but without large overhead expenses. I did not incur long-term debt from financial institutions that I would have to repay. I budgeted for each project, then hired and paid for the services. Once completed, I moved down the list until I accomplished them all.

Do not try to accomplish everything at once. Prioritize your tasks and go down the list. Starting a business is one thing; following through is what matters. Do not burn yourself out and become discouraged. Eventually you will develop the skill to work smarter rather than harder. During networking interactions, I kept hearing from others that it's important to work smarter rather than harder, and for a while it did not make sense to me because I felt I had to chase everything that seemed like an opportunity. My thinking was that it can't be a bad thing to pursue all opportunities. Right? I finally understood what working smarter meant years later in my business. You'll read more about this in chapter 15.

Before investing money to start a project, be sure to research, ask about the success rate from previous clients, set a time frame, and establish an action plan. Have everything in writing. This is especially important when relying on someone else's services to accomplish your goals.

While preparing to launch the business, I was working on my first children's book, taking a writing course, and perfecting my craft. I had it in my mind that I would launch the business in conjunction with my book signing.

When you create a direction and stay focused on getting there, the next steps are to implement them. That is what I did. I was crystal clear on where I was and where I wanted to be. Once I knew that my book would be published in 2012, I used that as the launch date for the company. Since I knew that date on the timeline when the book would be completed, I could then work backward to correlate my goals to match the timetable. I worked on getting the business registered and licensed, the taxes filed, and the website designed. I created my logo and set out to find a graphic designer. Then I enhanced the website with graphics and pictures of the products I would sell.

To accomplish a successful launch, you must have a direction. Once you map this out, start executing the steps and this will make for a well-thought-out, successful business launch. In my case, I knew I would be hosting the launch party in my home. Therefore, I needed a guest list, invitations, products on hand to sell, and food and beverages to serve. Think of how you want your attendees to have a memorable experience so that they want to come back and buy from you.

I aligned the steps of building the business so that it would be completed by the time my book was published. My intention was to host a book signing and business launch simultaneously. I did so in a very inexpensive way, by hosting an at-home book signing and business launch party.

In 2012, *A Frog in Grandma's Cup* was published and introduced along with samples of my baked goods at the book signing and business launch party. After tasting my lemon bars, guests became instant customers and they spread the word among their friends and coworkers, and that was my breakthrough. They learned what a great baker I am and that my focus is creating healthy lifestyle habits. They tasted the quality of ingredients that set me apart from other bakeries. One customer led to the next, and thus, my bittersweet journey with lemon bars and literacy began with some real zest.

The demand grew and so did my revenue. The lemon bars became so popular that I renamed them Super Star Lemon Bars. My book became a favorite and an inspiration among readers with small children; those readers recommended it to their peers, and just like the Super Star Lemon Bars, my book sales increased.

I need to admit that when projects such as designing my logo and learning the steps to building a brand was too much for me to handle, I had moments where I missed my corporate life. But I was determined. I believe that you must bring your whole self to the table if you want to thrive in today's world. No matter what obstacles you face, you have the power to change your life. I went about building the foundation to get to where I am without having enormous operating business expenses. I built the business from scratch with a small budget, a basic website, two products, and zero employees. But I had a vision!

The tasks at hand in building the company were too much to handle at times because I was doing all the creativity, research, planning, and implementing by myself. I was making a great change in my life by starting a business. The projects involved were a lot to handle while also managing a household. These were the times I reflected on my life in New York and missed the corporate world.

I had my two young children to still focus on, so I couldn't dedicate 100 percent of my time to the business. I had to learn how to find a balance, and that was difficult because the demands came from all sides in raising a family along with all that was required to start the business.

That's why shifting to piecemealing the process kept me going and kept me sane. Everything that I'm sharing in this book, I've learned the hard way. Now you can embrace piecemealing and not overwhelm yourself, like I did.

I had no brochures or printed materials for the business when I launched, and that was justifiable initially. The challenge was that I had confusing, rambling marketing messages which led to slowing sales. Then after I changed how I viewed the conditions and circumstances and applied some techniques that I'm sharing in this book, I strengthened my message and my vision. As a result, I've grown my business to success within its ten-year mark and defeated entrepreneur's remorse.

I want the same kind of success for you. I don't want you to have owner's remorse.

When life gave me lemons, I made Super Star Lemon Bars and promoted literacy. It is my hope that when life gives you lemons, you can know you've avoided a few of them through learning from my challenges.

Recipe for Success:

Avoiding Owner's Remorse

Break up overwhelming projects
into smaller bites.

Prioritize based on what is
urgent and important.

Don't allow others to convince you that
you must do everything at once.

Set budgets for everything
you are doing.

Don't feel you must go into
significant debt to start the business.

I built the business from scratch
with a small budget, a basic website,
two products, and zero employees.
But I had a vision!

Chapter Five
A Dash of Everything

n the early days after my launch, I began to form my web of connections through networking, which made me think that I had this high-flying career until I found out that there are risks that come with networking; that is something I had not really anticipated or considered.

The busy schedule of attending meetings and networking made me feel as if I was a scaled business. Every day, I'd get dressed in business attire, meet with folks, and hand out business cards. It was this activity that made me feel I had a high-flying career.

I spent most of my days networking and investing time and money into organizations and companies without achieving the results or benefits expected. Through my initial networking days, I had some painful, frustrating, and costly experiences. I will share some ridiculously embarrassing stories, only for you to better understand what I needed but didn't receive from these organizations I joined. Some organizations were primarily social, but I didn't know that at the time. I joined some that felt promising to meet my needs for customers, business growth opportunities, and flourishing marketing techniques that would yield me big financial gains, and yet they didn't. These were mistakes I made and learned the hard way.

In retrospect, if I knew then what I know now, would I still have the same experiences? Definitely not.

Some of what I've encountered from networking stemmed from being excluded in conversations and not feeling welcome in the group. One day while attending a meeting of an organization in which I was a member, I had an epiphany as I looked around the room filled with other members. I asked myself, *What am I doing here?* and I mentally evaluated my current situation. *I'm invisible to these women. I must stop riding a stationary bike expecting to move. As a businesswoman I have a limited amount of time, so I need to be deliberate and intentional about getting things done.* My days were stacked with these so-called meetings, traveling up and down the highways with the intention to connect, build relationships, and grow my business, but it was not bringing me the success I desired.

In that moment I discovered that I was not being true to myself. There were some things that were underlying hindrances to my growth, but I'd kept these hidden just to fit in because I did not want to fall into making excuses or being a victim. So I kept showing up and trying to fit in on other people's terms instead of just being me. Some of the things I tried to keep hidden included being a minority woman and a woman of color, having an educational background from another country, allowing others to overlook or not acknowledge my point of view, and believing that I must be this polished corporate person to be a good fit.

Well, guess what? This does not work in the corporate world either, so why did I believe it would work in the small business world? I had worked in corporate, but nobody realized this. I tolerated this treatment from others because I felt that I did not have the polished American education, though I did my best to acquire as much education as I could afford when I moved here. I did not have the family lineage or a wealthy network of people to help me do anything. Some people assumed that I was this wealthy, silver-spoon-in-my-mouth business owner. I was amazed by the assumptions that were made about me without even talking to me and getting to know me. I disregarded all of this because I felt the need to fit in.

Being a minority woman—yet purposely ignoring the fact that being a minority woman of color played a part in my decisions to surround myself with authentic, diverse people—I was sacrificing a part of who I was and the cultural diversity I loved. Instead, I pretended that the issue was not affecting me with the hope of being in the same classification of non-minority women.

Having an educational background from another country was challenging because of the way I interpreted several conversations or pieces of information due to the different ways education is taught. I was surrounded with fear and thought I would be seen as a bit weird or that others wouldn't quite understand. These women would speak about their education and talents that were completely different from my experiences. This is how they overlooked my point of view during conversations. It felt as though my knowledge and talents weren't as important as theirs.

I felt that to show my brilliance, I must be a polished corporate person; otherwise, they will not take me seriously. I decided to adapt to their behavior and act like them. And guess what? That was when they took notice of me. It was also at that time that I felt more comfortable pushing back whenever I felt dismissed. I was no longer putting my back against the wall. I was engaging and sharing my thoughts and perspectives, whether they were invited or not.

I am the type of person who makes the best of every situation and always try to put my best foot forward. My family members have all been planners, and by implementing that behavior into my personal and business decisions, we have enjoyed a lifestyle that we can afford. We travel, we invest, and as some would say, we are "always well put together."

When people assumed I was wealthy or privileged, they didn't know the hard work and sacrifices that were made to achieve that success. They saw the result rather than the work behind it all. They immediately assumed that I had the wealth to run my company, and therefore I had it easy.

All this rambling was going through my head on that fateful day at that meeting when I asked myself, *What am I doing here?* And I gained clarity. I picked up my belongings, walked out of the room, and removed myself from the organization. I did not care that my membership fee was nonrefundable; I just knew I had to separate myself from the facade.

I think sometimes this happens to many women and especially women of color. In my case, I might have been trying to portray myself as polished in order to appear more corporate. Meanwhile, I was giving and not receiving. I was broken, tired, exhausted, and still not making the right connections or meeting my goals because I did not have the right mindset. I wasn't clear on my audience or what I truly wanted for my business.

I was caught in a malaise of giving, giving, giving. Giving my time to show up and assist other women's events at no cost.

Giving products as donations to help with their raffles. Giving my experience by being on their committees to help develop their businesses. Giving to worthy causes has its rewards—but when you are giving with a mutually agreed expectation of some reciprocal reward or benefit and then don't get it, that is another situation entirely.

Not receiving the support when it was my turn was disheartening and upsetting. These same people I would help were always unavailable to help with my events. They couldn't offer any of their services as gifts because their services were "too expensive to give away." They were not willing to share resources or information when I asked for help, yet they openly welcomed it from me. They did not keep their word of helping me to connect with possible prospects after they had already reaped the benefits from my giving.

Looking back, I realize that there is a bit of a hilarity in not knowing what the heck I was doing when it came to networking or not being clear on what my attendance would accomplish. It's okay to mess up because we can turn those blunders into lessons learned. It's like baking and cooking: there are no mistakes, just more snacks; and when you remake the recipe, the outcome is much better.

Being true to myself played a huge part in my success moving forward, and now I let people know that I am a woman of color with a unique heritage and amazing qualities. I am not a victim. I am a proud, small business owner who has had to bootstrap to get where I am.

What I have also realized is that every single person in the room walks in with an agenda, yet only a small percentage of us in that room are willing to truly appreciate your agenda and make it an intention. At some point you must stop being desperate and realize that no one is going to do anything for you without you putting in the time, energy, focus, and resources to achieve your goals. And that's a huge lesson I needed to learn as a business owner.

We can all make big things happen, but no one is going to do it for us. You must learn the intentionality of networking; but first you must know who your audience is before you go into the room.

My initial networking experiences weren't fulfilling for me, but when I look at the people I've met and what I've learned from them, I realize I have expanded my networking knowledge. If you find that you cannot do business with some of the delightful people you meet or don't really learn anything from them, but they have a great network of connections, then let that be your takeaway. Nothing is lost and now you can move on by being kind, having some grace, and going to a better place next time.

Networking as a business owner was a new world to me and some of the decisions I made did not go well. After recognizing my failures, I realized that I needed to work on understanding myself, defining my needs, and figuring out what success looked like to me.

In my early stages of networking, I met people who told me that I needed to exaggerate more about what I do and the services I offer in order to get noticed. I found this type of behavior to be dishonest and would not agree with that advice. I was encouraged to mislead customers about the quantity of products I could provide in order to close a deal. I was told to describe my business beyond its current successful state and claim it had a higher cash value. All of this went against my core values of honesty and integrity. Misrepresentation of my company would eventually tarnish my brand and products, leading to both financial loss and weakened credibility.

I realized that I became easily influenced and was pushed into a lifestyle that didn't represent who I am. This had to be changed. I noted all the values and morals that I live by, and I made a list of the goals and objectives I wanted to achieve. I even took a personality quiz that I found in a magazine during one of my hair stylist appointments. It's funny how those quizzes can sometimes be spot on. Some of the questions included, "You're in a room filled with people you don't know while waiting for a colleague. Do you sit in a corner with a drink? Do you pretend to be like the others in the room? Do you walk over to the food bar and start a conversation?" My answer was to walk over to the food bar and start a conversation. By recognizing what my natural tendencies were, I gained more confidence to be true to myself and how I am most comfortable being.

This realization also made me take a closer look at how I was spending my time. All I did over four years was go from one meeting to the next, collecting business cards and showing up at every event possible, without realizing that I was only investing time and money into an expensive social life. The way

I saw it at the time, I was back in the game of being in the glamorous corporate world, and I loved that feeling.

If you don't know what you are looking for and why you need it, you become a hamster on a wheel. Since I did not have much experience in networking, I believed everyone who invited me to attend events to get my name out there. We fall into the trap of expectation. We believe that if we are in a room with like-minded people that we will support each other and help get our businesses known. In many cases, that's not the result. This is when you find both authentic people and people who do not keep their word. You end up wasting your time and perhaps your money, if you had to pay to attend. As business owners, we are eager to sell, make money, promote our businesses, and get known in the community, so every networking event seems like an opportunity for that.

I was giving away my time and services and helping others grow their business by sharing my skills; I was giving away my products for free, hoping to gain visibility and customers. I grew tired and angry of being told to offer my services for free to gain exposure and get my name out there. The only thing I got from all that exposure was an ice-cold taste of reality! Be aware of these catchphrases: *gain exposure* and *get your name out there*. They come with a price. Unless you are getting something in return to help move your business forward, don't get distracted with those offers.

When networking isn't working, it is time to reassess. Here's what networking really is about: networking is making connections and introductions to reach your audience. You do this through organizations that attract those audiences. But if you're going to the wrong places with the wrong audience, you're going to waste your time and money and still not meet your goals.

What I learned is that I didn't ask the proper questions to know my intentions because at that time, I didn't have the right mindset. I didn't know what I needed from those networking organizations, so there's no way I could have received it from being there.

Stop overthinking and start acting on your goals. I stopped worrying about what may not work; instead, I concentrated on the value of what my business has to offer. I stopped doubting myself and started comparing where I was and where I am now to where I wanted to be.

For a while I considered my efforts a failure. But they weren't failures. They were mistakes, not failure. Failures are brutal. Mistakes you can learn from and then grow as a result, so it's good to know the difference. This was when I learned that I didn't have the proper intentions—and it had nothing to do with the organizations.

That's when I made the mindset shift. And that right there is what I call maturing through the process because I realized I was disappointed, angry, frustrated, and broke from my experiences. Part of my maturity also included taking responsibility and being accountable as to how I would address my frustrations. When we are honest with ourselves, we gain clarity and direction.

Rather than blaming others, it is important to analyze the situation and see where or what you could have done differently and what the outcome might have been. Very often, we allow our ego to take over rather than admitting mistakes and letting go—there is no need to take everything personally or to fear what the outcome might be.

The first thing to understand is that every networking organization exists for reasons that others need, and some groups may just not be what you need. The number one lesson I've learned is that it had nothing to do with the members; it was all me.

I determined I needed to become more intentional when it came to networking. It was in this moment of realization that I took a two-year break from networking—at least the way I had been doing it. I hope my experiences can now spare you from learning these hard and expensive lessons firsthand.

Recipe for Success:

Networking Done Right

Choose organizations that
align with your values and focus.

Prioritize groups whose members
represent your ideal target market.

When asked to give your offering for free,
negotiate reciprocal value that is
mutually beneficial.

Don't give away your products or services
without a clear and written expectation.

Get involved and engaged with the group,
always being true to yourself.

Chapter Six
Sugar-Coated Promises

While networking was one harsh reality I needed to better understand, another one was when to believe that people would do as they promised.

After successfully publishing my first children's book, I wanted to publish more children's books. One of my biggest delay factors in publishing my second book was something that could not have been anticipated, nor was it within my control. The publisher suddenly stopped communicating with me; after my research, I discovered they were no longer in business, took my money, and never told me they were closing. I had to quickly come up with a plan to retrieve my manuscript and find another publisher.

This caused a one-year setback of publishing my second book. While researching to locate an illustrator for this book, I started looking for other publishers. This was difficult because I wasn't sure who I could trust, but this experience taught me to ask different questions of future publishers, such as, What happens if your company decides to close? I had already implemented a backup plan should something like this happen again, with alternate publishers and illustrators available to assist if needed. I'd rather work with an in-house publisher locally than with out-of-state or virtual companies. Having local access boosted my confidence and gave me the ability to build a relationship with a real person.

Another frustrating situation that occurred was believing an accountant whose advice led to great financial loss and despair because she failed to educate me properly on the rules of withdrawing money from my IRA account and how that would affect my tax bracket. I did ask questions but trusted her answers because I felt she was the expert.

The sugar-coated promises—lemons in disguise—kept coming with my investments in several public relations and marketing businesses and in people I had met and hired through networking organizations. Again, I trusted and believed in them, but all I received was more work and wasted time. I constantly had to supervise them because they were not staying on task. I had to point out errors or fix the issues myself, often bringing to their attention aspects of our contract agreements that were not being followed. Finally, I cut my losses, fired them, and threw out the bitter rind of the reality of it all.

Then came the juiciest lemon of all. I was finally fitting in, or so I thought. I was making friends and building business relationships, only to find out that these people were not interested in me. They did not want to be my friend. They saw me as an asset for their business and hooked me by making promises of introducing me to potential customers and expanding my business opportunities.

Then once they benefited from me being their customer, giving away my products and services at no cost, or taking advantage of my skills, they would not respond to my emails or phone messages. And when we happened to meet in person, they had a pretentious style of conversation and would continue with the same deceitful behaviors.

I hired so-called experts to maintain my website and produce weekly marketing campaigns but was disappointed with the slow leads and sales. When it comes to experts, it is important to clarify in writing what services will be provided. The experts hired for marketing and website maintenance indicated that my leads would increase by week three and sales would go up. I was trusting, so I believed them. The outcome was that I had to end up micromanaging the work, correcting the grammar and tone of their marketing campaigns, and calling out website maintenance not being done, which cost me sales. The website was offline at one point, and I did not know. Going forward, I've learned to build in a habit of checking my website every morning to make sure it's operating.

I became an expert at knowing that everyone has their own agenda. To extend the lemon analogy: the lemons are good, but the pith is bad. When the zest and juice of lemons appear to be shiny and attractive, you want to invest in buying them. However, once the top shiny layer is zested, the next layer (known as the pith) is revealed, and that, my friend, is a bitter experience. You don't want to add that pith to your recipe.

I now know how to read the room, which is a skill I implement and practice when I attend any meetings or when I am about to have discussions with people I do not know. It is simple. I listen keenly and pay attention to what is being said. I do not immediately say yes. Instead, I process the information and let the person know that I will follow up with them after I have had time to consider. I do not make commitments on the spot. Something I now understand is that when we are in a room, we pick up the energy of our surroundings. Therefore, we feel energized—and at times, without really assessing our intentions, we commit to offers that seem possible, ready to invest time and money and even overschedule ourselves because we are hopeful. I control that energy now with my intentions.

What I learned (and could have done differently) was to ask more questions and be confident about what I was looking for. At that time, I was hesitant because I did not want to come across as someone who was prying into other people's business. I had a scarcity mindset. I am one who doesn't want to pry into other people's business, and I transferred that personal belief to my business opportunities, which brought me no success. The right people are more than happy to share how and what they are doing that is bringing them success.

I had these setbacks because I was lacking the mindset of an entrepreneur. I didn't know how to craft my message to attract the right audience, and I didn't know how to build a team who could act as my board of advisers. I didn't know how to choose the right people.

I listened to the advice and business pitches and fell victim to them. Every offer seemed sincere, and I said yes to them all. But I have since learned that these mistakes often lead to new directions, perhaps the ones we are meant to take. At that time, I didn't know this, and it cost me. I spent thousands of dollars on organizations and business providers that failed me.

As time went by, I learned that some people are not going to help you find a job or launch your business. They are not even going to help you find clients. It's not their role in life. But at that time, I had decided to have faith in someone besides myself.

Think about your life and what obstacles you might face in starting and running your business. How can you address these obstacles, and who might be able to help you? Build a team who can help you achieve more than you can alone. You may not have the resources to hire employees, but teams come in many forms. Think about them as your board of advisers or strategic partners. They could be mentors, advisers, other cofounders, and subject matter experts who can help with ensuring your success. Choose people who you can count on to give good advice, feedback, and moral support.

I now know that to have faith in others starts with having faith in yourself—because then you know more clearly what you want and how they can best help you. You also know what you don't want and what you won't tolerate. And once all of this is understood from within, your choices and outcomes align to your goals and correlate to your bottom line as well.

Recipe for Success:

Choosing Experts and Collaborative Partners

Get in writing whatever is promised.

Set clear timelines and deliverables.

Confirm mutually agreed
upon expectations and outcomes.

Get references and actually
reach out to them.

Trust your gut instinct.

I needed to stop minimizing my worth. *If you want to be taken seriously,* then you must first show that you *value yourself.*

Chapter Seven
Slowing to a Simmer

While my launch seemed like a foolproof plan, there were bumps in the road. There were some things that did not go according to my plan. I was consumed with work; my baking schedule left me with little time for my family; and having to create a new work–life balance was a challenge. I felt frustrated, overwhelmed, and sometimes anxious. Things were not working out the way I'd hoped, and I wasn't enjoying the process. I had to rethink my strategies.

Having to work in a shared commercial kitchen was turning out to be difficult. The other tenants using the space were limiting the hours of operation in which I could bake, which impacted my sales. When circumstances are out of your control, as in this case of having to rely on the kitchen manager and accommodating others' schedules in order to produce, life becomes more challenging and frustrating instead of convenient as I had hoped.

Another challenge I endured was the struggle to find the right words to effectively describe the business and all I do. I knew my business had more potential than my bottom line would indicate. I just didn't know how to express that in meaningful, compelling words.

I pressed the pause button and did a business review, diving into my struggles and reviewing what was working and not working. I quickly realized that I was not aligning myself with the right people.

I stepped away from networking and social media and paused all office work. I used the time to carefully review all I was doing so far, noting what was working, what I felt pressured into doing, and what my investments of time and money yielded. I gained clarity and direction from this exercise. This helped me to create a direction leading to a real destination instead of an imagined one.

The key component that came out of this review was that I needed to stop minimizing my worth. If you want to be taken seriously, then you must first show that you value yourself. If your business is product-based and you're asked for samples incessantly, let your audience know that it cost you time and money to provide those "samples." Not every sample is or should be free. However, depending on the circumstance and the organization, you might consider having them document your product offering as a donation and ask them to please not refer them as samples. That term minimizes your product. By asking that you receive documentation for your product donation, you may get a charitable tax deduction for the value of the goods if it is a 501(c)(3) nonprofit. This does not work the same way with other types of nonprofit organizations or services being donated, so check with your tax accountant to be sure.

My approach is that products can be offered at a discounted price, but they should never be offered for free unless there is a charitable aspect. Donations can be effective to give away a certain amount or limited number of products. Budget what you are comfortable giving as a charitable contribution and what you are comfortable giving at a discount. Don't say yes to everyone or feel bad when you say no. Depending upon the organization or company, your donation could be gaining an advertisement in their newsletter promotion or giving you the ability to share about your business with others at a meeting. Everything doesn't have to be a financial exchange, but giving and receiving must always be a win-win situation in business.

I analyzed my habits and weaknesses and implemented a mind-your-own-business strategy where I stopped pleasing people and focused on doing what I needed to do in order to make me happy and successful. I don't mean that I became a snob or was not willing to help others. I found a way to win at life by letting go of trying to solve all the problems for others while neglecting myself. Instead, I focused on actions that would move my business forward and make me happy. I defined what I needed and what I should do to make progress.

I took a break from networking to determine where I wanted to be and what I needed to do to get there. As mentioned earlier, I stopped networking for two years, spending that time being strategic in my planning and implementation. This break afforded me the time to create additional products and increase sales with my existing customer base.

I came up with new ideas to grow the company, and I was able to hire an assistant. I adjusted my business plan to reflect more realistic goals. The types of goals I had previously set were lofty and unrealistic for what I had the capacity to do at the time. Building a one-million-dollar company and expanding into franchises were not the right fit at that time. Practical goals like increasing net income by the third quarter or getting books into several bookstores were more achievable. I talk more about goals in chapter 12.

I shopped around and interviewed business owners before selecting who to work with. My many poor choices in the past led me to hire so-called marketing and business-growth gurus and to lose money for services I believed would help me skyrocket to great income, yet didn't.

Once I became comfortable addressing my failures, the clearer I became on why I have this business and why I want to do it, which enabled me to attract the clients, projects, opportunities, and purchase orders that would lead to my success.

My "why" when I started the business was to provide products and services that would make a difference in people's lives. I knew there was a need for what I had to offer. I wanted to do this so that I could help others while making an impact in the community and the environment. I care about people and the planet, and I strive to add value wherever I live, making that place better than I found it.

Once I focused on my why, I was motivated to use my creative skills and expertise to work with the intention of increasing my company's visibility. When I expanded my products and notified my subscribers, the orders started coming in. Eventually my customers started sharing contact names and resources to help me expand my customer base; and soon my baked goods were in coffee shops, and my children's books were in schools.

My why also helped me come to terms with why I really started the business. It was to create a lifestyle that would allow me to utilize my expertise, passions, and creative skills that were never used before in the form of developing an amazing company that would allow me to be at home with my children while still working.

I also decided during this time of reflection to stop comparing. Comparing my business to others' businesses was detracting me from my own mission. Instead, I focused on being different by being creative and outthinking my competition.

The first step to this was to stop comparing my business to the big box stores and small storefront brick-and-mortar cafés. I chose to stand out rather than fit in with the rest. I focused on what customers really want and took an honest look at what the competition offers and doesn't offer. I saw the increased need for healthy eating, but customers were getting short-term solutions. I have long-term solutions, and that was my competitive advantage. I don't provide diets that people cannot maintain. I show them that healthy is not a diet; it's a lifestyle habit that needs to be created.

It wasn't until I invested in a business class and learned how to put these key factors in place that I was able to properly craft my message. Customers engage with you through your message. Your message is the main idea you want to communicate about your business. It should focus on how your product or service solves the customer's problem and benefits them.

I also learned in my reflection that not everyone is your customer, so don't be discouraged when someone tells you that your prices are too high, unfollows you on social media, or unsubscribes from your email list. You must know your worth and the value you offer. It took me a long time to get to this point because I was focusing more on having the orders and pleasing the customers, rather than making it right for both of us.

If you were to look at me today, I am known as several things. I'm a founder and CEO of a business, a wife, a mother, a caregiver, a celebrity chef, an award-winning author, and a philanthropist. I'm also known as the Lemon Bars Lady with boundaries because I am no longer a people pleaser. To even the casual observer, I appear independent and self-confident, comfortable with conflict and with expressing my needs. This behavior, especially coming from a woman, can evoke an accusation of selfishness and a few other choice descriptions I won't mention here, but you can probably imagine them. I'm not selfish, nor am I any of those other descriptions one might envision. Who I am is someone who takes seriously my mental health, my energy capacity, and my worth. For example, now when I'm approached with sales offers or requests that do not fit my needs or wants, I no longer say yes because I feel obligated. Instead, I gracefully say something like this, "Thank you for thinking of me. This offer is not what I need, so I'm going to pass."

This time pausing helped me get clearer about my business, what it needed, and what I needed, as well as what the marketplace needed to know and hear about my business. I realized that it really came down to knowing myself and my business better from the inside out.

Recipe for Success:

Crafting Your Message

Why should someone want to be your customer?

What about your product or
service would spark their interest?

What does the customer need to know,
and what's most important?

What sets you apart from the competition?

Why should a potential customer choose you?

How will your message make
the customer trust you?

Chapter Eight
Cream Rises to the Top

After I pressed the restart button, my business grew during this next phase; eventually I came to the point where I felt comfortable to walk into the bank and open a business account. I operated out of my personal account initially because banks at the time had requirements for business accounts that made it less attractive for a start-up. Their demands for high account balances in order to avoid fees and maintain the business account were not in my favor at that time. This is still a problem for many small business owners who want to minimize fees but cannot afford a large account balance.

When I opened my account, I was not interested in a business loan. I focused first on building a relationship with the bank. Within six months, I was offered a business line of credit with zero interest for one year and a low interest rate after that first year.

As the business continued to thrive, some tasks became overwhelming. Since I had properly positioned my finances, it allowed me to hire an assistant to help with some of the tasks that would free up my time to focus more on taking the business to the next level. I interviewed and hired a virtual assistant at a budgeted rate. Being specific about my needs when doing the hiring helped me stay within budget. In my case I budgeted four hours of work per month to assist with tasks such as researching information and newsletter topics, creating flyers, and working on other minor tasks that would normally be time consuming.

I have taught my children, "You get what you tolerate." In other words, if you accept unfavorable actions and situations, then you must abide by the results. For example, if someone frustrates you, and you do not find a way to let them know, they will continue to do it because you are tolerating it. Once I strongly made that my theme, it led to many wonderful milestones in all the relationships that I nurtured from that point forward.

With a new mindset and strategies in place, I grew my business exponentially within one year. By early 2014, my financial gains allowed me to go from having a home office to a leased office in the downtown Concord area. I invested in several reputable marketing and public relations businesses, and I increased my bakery products line to almost two hundred items.

By summer, I had completed and published my second children's book, which became a featured choice selection by the publisher AuthorHouse, at the BookExpo America at the Javits Center in New York City. My book sales were going well, and I was receiving book signing opportunities, attending book festivals, and making author appearances. During a vacation trip to London, I had the opportunity to introduce my books and line of business to some local shops. I stayed laser focused on growth and financial gain.

I also spent a portion of my time volunteering and being involved in the community. Being involved in the community is important because it helps you connect to your community and make it a better place. If you want to thrive and let people know about your business, become involved. Dedicating your time as a volunteer helps to make new friends, expand your network, and boost your social skills, especially when you're in a new place (as I've experienced).

I got involved with a Rotary Club to offer my children's books as a part of my raising literacy awareness, which ties to my business. I volunteered at schools for authors' day and empowered girls to be leaders. I helped with Girl Scout troops, animal shelters, and homeless shelters. To determine my volunteer involvements, I chose what I am most passionate about and aligns with my mission.

I managed volunteering so it was balanced with business activity by inquiring what their upcoming events and needs were so that I could factor in the time, and it wouldn't affect my business activity. Also, if I couldn't commit to be at the event for the entire time, I would volunteer for a shorter period so that I could get back to work. And if I couldn't attend at all, I would send someone else in my place—a staff member, family member, or friend.

However, as the saying goes, with success comes failure, and I was about to experience that in many forms. It seemed like everything that could possibly go wrong went wrong! What life has since taught me is to be prepared to be completely unprepared. I was basking in the progress I was making—until 2016 turned into the year I hired the wrong people, overinvested, and followed the wrong advice.

Recipe for Success:

The Power of Pausing

Don't force anything. Simply reflect first.

Allow yourself to be in the moment.

Define your needs versus your wants.

Don't panic. Your thoughts create your emotions,
and your emotions create your actions.

Being involved in the community
is important because it helps you
connect to your community
and make it a better place.

Chapter Nine
Burnt around the Edges

n 2016, I was introduced to a restaurant owner who had a lovely area for a coffee shop. This was my ideal dream and the right move to make, and I invested in the business. I purchased all the equipment and supplies needed and had my signage made; my husband and I painted and refreshed the space. I sent out invitations for opening day in preparation for Christmas holidays.

Ten days before opening day, we received a letter from city hall indicating that all the shops in the area must move because they were going to demolish those buildings and begin construction of a baseball stadium. When I picked up my city permit a few weeks before, no one informed me about that plan. The owner and other owners had no previous long-term notice either. The city gave others enough time to relocate, but I couldn't afford the rent where those businesses were going.

I remember going through several levels of emotions, from sadness and anger to defeat and hopelessness. I was devastated as I processed why this was happening to me. It felt like yet another setback was happening to me. I asked myself, "Why am I trying so hard, yet every climb up throws me back down?" And I was beginning to question, "What's the point of continuing?"

Hanging Up My Apron

At that moment, I decided I was done being a businesswoman. I was exhausted building a dream that I was starting to believe was not meant to be. All the negative voices came out with reasons why I should push the stop button and let go of being an entrepreneur. I was not respected when I told people that I was an entrepreneur because they did not see this as a business; they saw it as a hobby or pastime. This is one of the misnomers about having a lifestyle business: it is "not really a business."

All that was left for me to do was cut my losses and move on. My husband helped me to remove the sign and pack up my supplies. To this day, the sign sits in my garage as a reminder of my resilience. I cannot use it because I've rebranded my business ever since.

Thus 2016 was the year of brutal lessons learned. Not only did I invest and lose on the storefront, but my accountant failed to give me proper advice on taking money from my 401(k) investments to support my business throughout 2016. Because of that, I ended up owing more in taxes and did not have any refunds. Talk about adding salt to the wound. I had to end my office lease and move back to my home office. I was crushed because at that time this was how I was measuring my success.

I made the decision to step down from being a business owner and go back to searching for a corporate job. Then something changed my mind. Every New Year's Eve I reflect on the year and write down successes and losses; instead of making resolutions, I make a list of goals to guide me through the upcoming year. I find this to be more realistic and no pressure.

When I faced adversity, I did allow the pressure to get to me in the moment. We all do that sometimes. However, there were times when I had to keep a level head and push past the devastation to arrive at success with some strategies.

Resetting the Table

For me, it was about clearing what was no longer working, including removing the debris of things I had no control over. This process of clearing is something you can also use to get your head back into a place of reenergizing your faith in yourself and your business.

- **Clear the table:** I removed all the things that brought me disappointments by creating a worksheet listing problems and solutions. Then I wrote down what I did, what didn't work, and how I intend to fix them. This action helped me see how to plan and do things better.

- **Clear the energy:** I let go of my anger and pity. I wrote down what my weaknesses were and how I reacted to them. Once I did this, I gained clarity and found better ways, such as rethinking how to manage my disappointments.

- **Clear the clutter** I evaluated who and what wasn't moving me toward success. I ended relationships and disconnected with the people and businesses who brought me no value. Once I let go of the guilt of these obligated relationships, it opened space for me to spend more time developing the business and more rewarding relationships. I no longer had to justify my reasons for saying no. People come into our lives for different reasons, but not everyone is meant to stay. I practice this thought whenever I am faced with an unpleasant or unhealthy experience.

- **Clear the mindset:** I quit thinking that my work was just a paycheck and stopped internalizing other people's interpretation that my work was just a hobby. I focused on the fact that this was a successful business with big success done my way. I stopped considering myself as "small" and changed the way I introduced myself to other businesses and corporations when promoting my services to them. I spoke confidently just as I did when I worked in corporate and represented those companies.

Creating a business can feel like baking bread that never rises. My life felt like I was caught in a cake that was collapsing. I kept trying to climb out, only to reach the top and fall back down and start over again. I felt like Rocky Balboa in those *Rocky* movies: losing the fight, being beaten, yet still going back into the ring.

Just like burnt, deflated bread where the crust is pulled down by gravity and collapses, those words are pretty much how I summed up 2016.

As I reflected on the year, I was reminded that I've been at the bottom before, and I know the way back up; it is through resilience and fearlessness. It also occurred to me that I really do not want to go back to a corporate job. I had left that world behind, and I could either work for a company and grow their vision or run a company where, even though I will face challenges and might not have all the answers, I would still know what I want and what success would look like for me.

A few things came to mind as I did my review, but one stood out the most. Maybe I was overconfident and wasn't looking at the big picture of where my finances were distributed or wasn't detecting the pattern of my commitments. I was merely focusing on scaling the business with every idea that seemed right. The big picture became clear of where I was misguided: impulsive spending on every idea that business owners told me to try. I was blinded with the thrill of scaling the business.

I was exhausting my energy and money because I was not getting the results I expected, and that behavior affected the joy of building my company. I also realized that entrepreneurship is a marathon, not a sprint. And the finish line may look different depending on your goals. You will have countless hurdles to jump, but this is what it means to be in business. Therefore, you must create your own direction or others will help you stay lost.

Sometimes, letting go of what makes us uncomfortable often leads to marvelous experiences. So I let go of my anger, frustrations, and failures, and decided to make a conscious decision to focus on strategies to rebuild the company.

Recipe for Success:

Building Versus Scaling a Business

Create your own direction;
don't let others sway you.

Let go of who or what
makes you uncomfortable.

Have the courage to
get out of your comfort zone.

Make conscious decisions based on
clear goals, objectives, and budget.

Focus on building a better business
versus scaling it.

Entrepreneurship is a marathon,
not a sprint.
And the finish line may look different
depending on your goals.

Chapter Ten
The Dough Rises Again

Staying laser focused with monthly goals and assessments kept me moving closer to achieving what success looked like for me. At the end of 2017, I had accomplished my goals and recovered from the pitfalls of 2016. While writing my goals on New Year's Eve, I decided it was time to refresh with a new beginning, and so in 2018, I rebranded the business with a new name and logo.

I did this by changing my approach to how I processed ideas and information that could lead to possible growth. In the past, I would make a to-do list with everything that needs to be done and attempt to accomplish them all at once. However, I would not get the desired results because some tasks were left unfinished; some were completed, but I was not taking that completion to the next level to yield success. I had forgotten the brilliance of my piecemealing methodology that helped me get my business off the ground in its beginning.

I realized I needed help, so I hired a professional website designer to create a new website expanding my content and updating a variety of bakery products. I leveraged the value of one of my children's books by creating a Read-and-Learn Bingo Game, along with hiring an educator to create lesson plans to enrich my approach when presenting my offers to schools and day care centers.

Because I was feeling better grounded, I also managed my finances more wisely. When I invested capital into creating the Read-and-Learn Bingo Game, my graphic designer and a retired teacher were hired to manage the project. Upon completion of my trademark, I pitched the game to day care centers and elementary schools and they became instant customers. At book signings, these became added assets to my sales revenue.

I sought new opportunities by taking self-taught online masterclasses to enhance my skills, and I removed myself from the distractions of social media that was not adding value to my growth. I wanted to be productive and intentional. I focused on my goals, planned out my tasks, and executed them. This practice brought growth and gave me a public business presence later on.

When I became more knowledgeable and thoroughly prepared, I stepped back into the entrepreneurial world. That took me a year—and this time, I was much wiser. I chose the people I wanted to network with and the clients I wanted to work with. I chose the customers I wanted to serve. I was no longer giving away my labor, time, and products for free. There was no more begging for business or ice-cold tastes of reality from getting my name out there for visibility and not reaping the expected sales. Customers were locating me after learning about the quality of my products and services, and my credibility.

Throughout the year, business growth and revenue continued to flourish, and I was now in a good place where I could invest in publishing a third book. I wanted this to be a cookbook with healthy recipes. My plan was to use this to expand in a different way that still aligned with the vision and mission of the company.

Growing your business is *your* business. Learn all you can about the functionality of your business so that if your assistant leaves, you can still get the job done. I had the experience of losing my assistant of four years when she changed careers and would no longer be in my line of work. Fortunately, I was brushing up on my technical and media skills, which allowed me to maintain my website and other applications without setbacks. I was able to hold down the fort while going through the hiring process for a new assistant.

Be disciplined and intentional in knowing the value of your work and build that respect. This includes being intentional when socializing. I politely let my friends and family know that my schedule was very complex and my social time was limited. I didn't want to commit to things then have to cancel, so I asked for their understanding and support, especially during the starting years and when I was facing challenges.

Assessing your networking is an ongoing need. Is it working for you? Evaluate whether the organizations, businesses, and colleagues are helping you move toward your destination. However, that is not the only aspect of your business you should be assessing on an ongoing basis. Every aspect of your business requires your attention to make sure it is as you had hoped and intended.

This is why strategic planning is so important. For me, strategic planning is the process of documenting and establishing a direction for your small business, as well assessing where you are and where you are going. As a small business owner, you have a better idea of the goals and objectives you want to accomplish when you have a strategic plan in place because you have a clear vision and plan for where you are headed.

Here's what your strategic plan should include, based on the template I developed and used for my business.

Competitor Analysis	Vision
Offerings and Distinctions	Mission
Pricing and Costs	Core Values
Ideal Target Audience	Short-Term Goals
Location and Access	Long-Term Goals
Problem Solving	Action Plan
	Quarterly and Annual Review

Provide an overview of your business, where it is now, and include the time frame you're looking at in the strategic plan. Within that overview, include research on competitors, what makes your offerings distinctive, the pricing and costs, along with who is your ideal market and the problem or problems you are solving. When it comes to cost and operations, confirm how you will find your suppliers. This planning will verify if there is a need for what you are offering.

When looking at problems solved, you should also look at trends because those can lead you to understand a problem that is being overlooked. Looking at your business location and access is also important. I was innovative in determining that my café could be online initially. That was unheard of at the time. So don't be afraid of doing something different just because it hasn't been done before.

Next, when you look at your vision and mission, does it align with your industry or does it disrupt it a bit? Your vision and mission are part of what will set you apart, so it is important to spend some time on this along with your core values.

Every strategy is unique to the business it is serving. Keep this in mind. While every strategy should have key components, how it plays out is very different for each business. That is what makes being an entrepreneur so exciting and challenging all at the same time.

Recipe for Success:

Why Strategy is Important

Strategy…

Allows quarterly and midyear business
reviews to be based on benchmarks
that measure your growth;

Helps you figure out what is not working;

Determines what you are tolerating
or doing that needs to be changed;

Helps you better understand your destination
and what it will take to realize your vision;

Assesses your biggest customers and how to keep
them while attracting more like them.

Every aspect of your business
requires your attention
to make sure it is as you had hoped
and intended.

Chapter Eleven
A Pinch of Perspective

Overcoming the scarcity mindset that often holds us back from growing our business is a big hurdle for many business owners to leap. It certainly was for me. Through my coaching experiences I learned that a scarcity mindset can make us think that we don't have enough. In most cases, it comes down to money, so we hold off growing our business because we believe we do not have the money to spare. When I shifted that thinking and instead recognized that there was enough money (even if not a whole lot), suddenly there was enough for me to invest in the business. Rather than being afraid to use it, I started to see the cash in the account as a resource for reinvesting in the business.

I also made the conscious effort to change my scarcity mindset to an abundance mindset by surrounding myself with positive people, and I focused on opportunities instead of limits. I stopped worrying about money; instead of being afraid to implement new ideas for growth, I took the chance because I had the right mindset and was more confident now.

It was because of hiring a coach that I was able to shift my mindset. I'll share a funny story with you so that you understand how much of a squirrel I was, running around all day trying to find a nut—that is, before I got perspective from a coach.

When I had my first meeting with my business coach, she asked if I had a schedule. I replied, "Of course, I have a schedule. Take a look!" I might have even scoffed a little as I showed her my planner stacked with all sorts of meetings and events. My days were filled with traveling to different places. When she saw that, I could tell that this was not a schedule. As she looked at what I presented to her, she adjusted her necklace; the next thing we saw was the broken necklace with beads rolling across the floor of the restaurant in all directions.

I gasped and immediately got on my knees, crawling around trying to grab them. That was my comedy show, and we joked about how the magnitude of my ridiculous chart which I thought was a schedule pulled her necklace apart. It also seemed rather symbolic in how I was scattering myself too thin and allowing my so-called schedule to control me rather than to serve me.

That was when I learned how to properly set and utilize my schedule. I found it a bit challenging initially because I was used to doing everything all at once. But by creating this new habit, the results were rewarding. At first, it was hard for me to see a schedule as a tool with blocks of time; it had previously been more of a to-do list to work through, but that approach had kept me jumping and had resulted in several unfinished tasks each day.

I was previously the "do it all and get it out of the way" person with mostly unsuccessful results. I would start my day with nothing else in mind but knocking out a long list of work tasks to do before 4 p.m. so that I could be available for my children when they returned from school. I made phone calls to connect with people I had met and sent emails to satisfy others—I was always trying to get tasks done. Yet at the end of the day when I looked back, all I was doing was shuffling tasks around and making no real progress toward success. Needless to say, I was a squirrel running around; I was becoming exhausted, anxious, and irritated because I was not getting the tasks completed. I was trying to get everything done quickly. But after learning from my coach how to implement manageable work habits, I learned how to create a true schedule that focused on being efficient and effective.

Being accountable and working with the strategies my coach helped put in place, I became focused and knew how to use my time more effectively. I used the tools given to help me figure out cost of goods sold, and I learned the right formula to make this task simpler. I learned how to set my weekly and daily schedule by blocks of time, which I had not been doing before. That was very productive. I was seeing success in my work.

At this stage, I was educated enough to continue on my own. My coach even said I was ready to apply all the skills I was taught. With the guidance, tools, and lessons from my coach, I had a better understanding on how to work smarter.

What I also learned through this process is not to be afraid to make scary decisions. Growth sometimes requires doing something a little risky. I risked hiring a business coach despite hearing stories of other people's failures with coaches. When I was advised against hiring a coach, I focused on my purpose and knew the right questions to ask. I also knew when it was time for me to function without that continued support, and finding the right coach reaffirmed this when it was mutually agreed I could now handle things on my own.

With some naysayers discouraging me from hiring a coach, I was determined that if properly selected, I would not have the negative experiences others had with coaches. Here are the questions and expectations I considered as I prepared to choose my coach.

- What is your expertise?
- What industries have you coached?
- What do you do best?
- What additional skills besides coaching can you add to bring me value?
- How much experience do you have?
- What are your values?
- Can you share testimonials from past clients?
- What is your success rate for coaching?
- How long have you been a business coach?
- What are your credentials? Are you certified, and what types of training do you have?
- What is your business coaching style? Do you coach with the focus of helping me find my own answers, or do you operate like a consultant who gives me answers and opinions?

The key is to know what you want out of a coach. You might want accountability or someone to brainstorm with who will give you their honest opinions. You might want a business coach with skills in areas you are still learning, such as marketing, sales, or operations.

When my coaching sessions ended, I continued what I learned to move forward and increase revenue. I had created the foundation of healthy work habits that helped me perform better, be more creative, and connect effectively by positioning myself for success through being consistent in what I do with my work and investing my energy to further my growth—knowing what I want when I walk into a networking group or meeting, knowing how much work I can take on, knowing when to say yes and when to say no without doubting myself.

It was because of my coaching sessions that I changed my approach, and the results have been significant. A coach also helped me in knowing how to better set goals. Since then, I am setting goals and achieving them. In the next chapter, I will share how.

Recipe for Success:

Successful Coaching Experience

A quality coach…

Takes an interest in you and what you're doing;

Guides you toward your goals without
getting discouraged;

Helps you discover the gaps between where
you currently are and where you want to be;

Combines real life and work experiences
and doesn't coach from a textbook;

Has the ability to diagnose
specific issues in your business;

Holds you accountable to implement
the solutions to get real results.

What I also learned through this *process is not to be afraid* to make scary decisions. *Growth sometimes requires doing* something a little risky.

Chapter Twelve
Goals Are Your Ganache

Without goals, you have nothing to hold your focus or business together. I say goals are your ganache because they are held together by your vision and mission for your company. Your vision and mission are what make your goals relevant and inspiring. Your vision and mission give your business a distinct flavor, and your goals help everyone get a taste of that in unique ways.

Setting goals is important, but very few of us (including me in the beginning) know how to properly set them. We end up self-sabotaging. We overcomplicate our goals. We create too many of them. We're unrealistic. We're too detailed. We waste our time. I was doing all these things, which meant I was performing my goal setting wrong.

I have two types of goals segmented by quarter and year. I set the quarterly goals at the beginning of each quarter and the annual goals at the beginning of the year. Then I focus on what I want to accomplish in the upcoming quarter and what I want to achieve by the end of the year. At the end of each period, I review the list, check off what was completed, and move the ones I did not accomplish to a new list for the next period.

Being intentional meant being more focused on how I was going to accomplish what I set out to do. I implemented a Goals Task Matrix, breaking my goals and tasks into four categories. Here is an example of some goals I have set that are reasonable and that can be quantifiably achieved using my Goals Tasks Matrix.

Goals Tasks Matrix

Do First: *Tasks that are critical, important, require immediate attention, and may be tied to deadlines.*

- Select four newsletter topics for the month
- Write for one hour daily
- Create cooking class lesson plans
- Increase cooking class attendance by three
- Walk and practice yoga at least two times per week.

Do Later: *Tasks that are still priority but are not tied to a deadline or to another important task.*

- Organize holiday book signing
- Plan holiday bakery menu
- Register for HSC fall gala

Delegate: *Tasks that you could possibly delegate to a reliable person. The tasks are still urgent but may require less attention.*

- Social media content posts
- PR research on media platforms for cooking shows
- Retail store contacts for spice blend

Postpone: *Tasks you would like to do but don't need to be done in the next quarter or year.*

- Idea for store front
- New projects or leadership roles
- Farmers market approach

You'll notice I include some personal goals because for a small business owner, goal setting does not stop with the business.

When the quarter ends, I can literally go through each of these goals and check off whether they've been achieved. They are easily measured so they are either completed or not. My goals for the whole year are similar, just on a bigger scale.

Goals Are a Recipe You Adjust

I have a confession to make. I often do not accomplish my goals. Sometimes things happen that get in the way. But I do not get nervous or upset; I just figure out why, and then reset for the next period. At least I know what I want to do, even if it doesn't get done that quarter or even that year.

Goal setting does not need to be complicated. Goals are just a list of stuff to get done and by when. When I was not achieving my goals, I realized that I had been overcomplicating my goal setting. I was creating these lofty, unquantifiable, and (in many cases) unreachable goals like "improve my company's branding" or "increase sales 110 percent" or "have a million-dollar company in three years."

I soon came to the realization that goals are really nothing more than tasks that you measure. I am just making a to-do list of stuff I want to make sure gets done by the end of a quarter or by the end of the year. That's it!

That's how you fix this problem. That's how you move forward. That's how you reach your goals.

Recipe for Success:

Goal Setting That Works

Consider your goals as tasks with a deadline.

Make them quantifiable and reasonable.

Establish them for a quarter and for the year.

Track and monitor progress.

If you don't achieve everything, don't fret.

Move open items to the next quarter or year.

I say goals are your ganache
because they are held together
by your vision and
mission for your company.

Chapter Thirteen
Setting the Timer

Time really is precious when you own a business. I know I don't need to tell you this. How do you make the most of your time and keep your sanity too? Over these years I have accumulated some best practices for what has helped me manage my time more effectively, and I hope it will do the same for you.

First, let's talk about distractions. Both social media and emails are big distractors. I set a specific time to deal with these. I also implement a "no social media" mindset when working on tasks, especially social media browsing rather than social media posting for my business. Being distraction-free also includes turning the phone on vibrate to avoid distracting phone calls.

We all get inundated with emails. Spend twenty to thirty minutes to stay on top of emails and instant messaging. Immediately delete those of no interest to you. Create and label folders, then place any messages that need responses and further actions where you can easily locate them; respond during your next block of time based on their priority.

Like my Goals Task Matrix, I also approach how I spend my time in a purposeful manner. Create a priority list, writing everything down for the day and week; that becomes your schedule of things to get done. Arrange your wake-up time, self-care tasks, phone calls, and emails into blocks of time. When it comes to your action-plan items, look at what must be done daily, weekly, monthly, and quarterly. I recommend taking some time on Sunday before your work week begins to schedule your time so you are ready to go on Monday. It is time well spent.

Just as your goals need to be reviewed, so does your progress in how your time being spent. Are you reaping what you are trying to achieve? I changed how I connected with others and approached my networking. Instead of being in several groups, I picked one that I felt confident would bring me good value for my investment. This kept me from being distracted with too much information and too many obligations. My past experiences with networking taught me that I tended to gather a lot of information in the form of business cards and brochures because I was hopeful that those would turn into business opportunities. Then once I returned to the reality of my office, that information became another layer on my to-do list; most of these pieces of information never came to fruition.

The decision to commit to one group as my resource for networking allowed me to hire a business coach to establish a direction on how to move the company forward, and I invested in a business structure for success. My time was better spent this way. I was no longer bouncing from networking meeting to networking meeting.

By sticking with one group, I remained focused on building relationships with the members and utilized resources and opportunities they provided.

Delegating effectively is a huge component to time management. The first time I realized the power of delegating to others was when I accepted my talents and decided my time was better spent where my talents were best used. I was investing too much time on small tasks such as drafting flyers or posts for social media, composing the newsletter, researching libraries, and other similar tasks. These small but necessary tasks were holding me back from working on developing the business. Quite often we think we will save time by doing everything ourselves and being in control. It's quite the opposite.

When you can separate your work and delegate to other employees, that is how you save time. What is important is making sure your assistants understand your voice, tone, and the way you communicate so that your customers know the content is truly coming from you. I created the topic with bullet points. My assistants generated drafts, I edited, and then they sent out the finished product. I was still in control but doing so by delegating, which took the pressure off me.

Another aspect of time management is learning how to say no. I no longer took on additional tasks that would negatively affect my goals, and I stopped saying yes to everything that I thought might lead to something successful. Although I liked doing some things, I eliminated them based on what value I was receiving, whether it was investing too much time to bake an elegant but unprofitable cake or feeling obligated to accept (at no charge) a speaking engagement that took a lot of preparation. I could be using that time to work on something else that yielded greater progress or opportunity for the company.

I stopped saying yes to everything by thinking it through first. What will it entail in time, money, resources, or stress? Am I overcommitting by accepting this? I focused on my intentions in everything I knew would require time. I would think before committing to meetings or events, and sometimes that meant less social time with friends. This came with a price. Several of my friends couldn't understand that I had less time to socialize and the reasons for that. It cost me some friendships, but it also helped me see who my true and supportive friends really were.

Friendships are important to me. True friends will support you through challenges and growth, not just the good times. Unfortunately, in some cases this didn't apply to everyone I thought of as my friends, and that made me sad. I understood their feelings of not getting to spend time together because they couldn't see the demands of my work and what it took to build a business since some of them were not business owners themselves. They either were working for a company or at home. I realized I needed to concentrate on what and who were a good fit for me.

I implemented a balanced schedule and stuck to it very strictly so that I didn't overwhelm myself. I created steps and tools to manage my schedule, time, and energy. I stopped multitasking and sneaking in household chores and family tasks during my work schedule. I created healthy work habits and quit trying to figure out every task at once. By doing so, I removed the high level of pressure and anxiety I had been previously putting on myself.

Focusing on getting one task completed before moving to the next can be challenging, especially when you have stacks of work to be done. However, focusing on *one* thing at a time will help you get through those stacks faster. It is a rewarding feeling when you know you've completed a task rather than worked on several tasks that all remain incomplete.

I looked for ways to stay organized, manage my schedule, and block time for tasks. Being intentional with my daily tasks extended into being intentional with what I wanted to accomplish weekly, monthly, and quarterly.

I even began to set timers for tasks. This has been quite effective at keeping me focused on what I am doing without getting distracted. I do not check my phone for messages or look up social media when I am working on my tasks.

All this time management led me to another realization: the importance of taking care of myself with healthy rituals and habits that nurture *me* and not just my business. More on this in the next chapter.

Recipe for Success:

Time Management Secrets

Set a timer to keep you focused.

Avoid procrastination.
Either do it or eliminate it.

Avoid distractions and
interruptions to your work

Set a schedule with boundaries.

Do one thing at a time. No multitasking.

It's okay to say no. Say no often.

Before you commit, pause and
consider what is expected.

Review your progress and adjust.

Being intentional with my daily tasks *extended into being intentional with* what I wanted to accomplish *weekly, monthly, and quarterly.*

Chapter Fourteen
Healthy Gulps of Sanity

As I mastered time management, I also realized that I was the master of nothing if I didn't take care of myself. It is easy to be overwhelmed, overworked, overcommitted, over everything when you own a business. More business owners suffer burnout because they don't realize the importance of taking care of themselves while taking care of their business.

I have realized the positive, nurturing effect of waking up early and keeping a morning routine so that I am ready and focused without getting burned out. I created healthy habits with a morning and evening routine. It involves how I start my day and batching my tasks for efficiency. Through time management I stopped being scattered and became more focused, which reduced my stress level.

By focusing on one thing at a time, getting it done, then moving on to the next task, I stopped allowing myself to be pulled in a myriad of directions. I took care to focus on my priorities first. If I had time left to spare, I assisted others. This is not being selfish. I used to think like that, then I realized others weren't making me a priority. You are who needs to make yourself a priority.

Creating a schedule that prioritizes what is most important to you is also part of taking care of yourself and your business. A schedule includes setting a start time, lunch break, and an end time—and sticking to it. Set office hours like a traditional job. Close your door if working from home so that you are not interrupted.

Take regular short breaks. I cannot emphasize this enough. Don't mix chores with office hours and consider that to be your break. Take a *real* break. Take five or ten minutes several times a day to get up and stretch; peacefully sip a cup of tea or coffee.

Think before committing to meetings or social events. Stop people-pleasing. Get all the worthless people out of your head who are causing drama, are naysayers, or are always making excuses.

Recognize when people are dumping energetic clutter on you. Energetic clutter may come in the form of complaining, speaking negatively of others, or speaking in ways that detract from joy or growth. This clutter is their responsibility to hold, not yours, so remove yourself from it.

Most importantly, remember how valuable you are to your business and your family; that's why taking care of yourself matters the most.

Recipe for Success:

Healthy Habits = Healthy You

Make yourself a priority.

Take five- to ten-minute
breaks throughout the day.

Be in the present;
notice and appreciate the little things.

Step outside for a breath of fresh air.

Quit trying to keep up with the "cool" crowd.

Allow yourself to do less and remove
the pressure you put on yourself.

Find peace by steering clear of negativity.

Chapter Fifteen
Fresh, Never Frozen

Business-changing breakthroughs can come in unexpected ways with challenges, experiences, and new viewpoints. In 2019, I became more confident in my decisions related to monetizing my business as I implemented revenue-generating services that would allow me to provide my multifaceted expertise.

As my presence grew, customers learned more about my specialty and what sets me apart from other bakers and chefs. I was given the opportunity to become a vendor at one of the area's well-known farmers markets. Being a vendor was new to me, but I said yes. I soon discovered that working at a farmers market is no easy job, especially when your products involve food. My days were consumed with planning, prepping, baking, and packing, plus waking up at 4 a.m. on Saturdays to complete the baking before driving fifty minutes to set up. Many people are not aware of the labor-intensive, behind-the-scenes work it takes; this may appear glamorous, but it takes a lot of effort and willpower.

The insight that changed everything came in unexpected ways from being at the farmers market. At first, I viewed the farmers market as not what I wanted; I would prefer a storefront. A storefront was how I was measuring success, and I felt that having a storefront would be fancy and elegant, bringing in lots of customers. This seemed glamorous compared to my presence at the farmers market, which I viewed as an unattractive way to sell. But once I viewed the process differently, it opened doors of opportunities as I built relationships with the customers.

One of those opportunities included meeting a TV news anchor from Charlotte's weekend morning show on WBTV, one of the top television stations in North Carolina. She came to the market to cover a story about the community. Funny enough, we met through my Super Star Lemon Bars. After she tasted one, she exclaimed that she had never tasted anything like it. When she learned more about my business concept of promoting healthy lifestyle through cooking, baking, and education, she invited me to be on their show as a chef and cookbook author who teaches healthy living practices in simple ways. Since then, I have been a resident chef of the WBTV-Charlotte station.

Moreover, I learned through my farmers market experiences how to finally work smarter. After laboring to produce goods and then be present at the farmers markets, I often would be frustrated by bringing home unsold baked goods. I realized I was wasting time and money to produce items I hoped would sell. So I decided to create a weekly market menu structured only to specific items. Then I added that list to my website and informed customers that they could preorder their products and pick them up at the market. Based on what they ordered, I would then bake those items because they were guaranteed sales. I would make a limited number of extras to sell at the market. This led to everything being sold out and no inventory to bring back. It was steps like this to work smarter, not harder, that yielded the results I wanted.

As another example, I created healthy work boundaries and committed to setting and sticking to them. This affected everything from my holiday baking hours to the items in inventory. Rather than taking every order that customers placed, sometimes at the last minute, I set ordering deadlines and held myself to them as well as others. This stopped me from running in circles and giving up family time to fulfill orders. I balanced my focus on sales by factoring in my needs as well.

In 2019, I again tested the waters of writing by completing and publishing my cookbook, *Just Eat: Pure and Simple Cooking.* This bold move opened doors of opportunities but also brought frustration from having to constantly defend my line of work. To many people, I was seen as an entrepreneur who was focused on too many things. I had many naysayers questioning why I would have a cookbook when my books previously were all children's books. I was told that I needed to focus on one product rather than doing several things simultaneously.

Yet this book created another stream of income, which was a key factor to my financial success during the COVID-19 pandemic. In the same year it was released, my cookbook won a Platinum MarCom Award. As I became increasingly visible to the public, more opportunities came to share my expertise on healthy eating, including speaking engagements and requests for to-go meals that opened additional streams of income.

More and more advance success for business engagements were happening, which made 2019 phenomenal. Growth allowed me to create job opportunities for two positions, and I hired a full-time bookkeeper as well as an administrative assistant who could also handle deliveries.

Throughout 2019, I continued to educate myself each day and to expand my own ideas on what it means to live my life with creativity and meaningfulness. I refreshed my business model recipe list, just as I would for baking and cooking.

Thus 2019 was a year of resilience and thriving, and it ended with great achievements that included a trip to Italy, finally fulfilling a goal I had set each year for over seven years. I was thrilled to mark it off my list as I did my year-end review. I had also increased the company's revenue with a 33 percent gross profit margin and was ready to dive into the new year.

I am a believer of the saying "everything happens for a reason." Everything I did in 2019 unexpectedly prepared me for something no one could have been prepared for—the COVID-19 pandemic.

It was my intention to complete this book in 2020, but once again, life tossed me stinging lemons with the COVID-19 virus that turned into a pandemic, leading to a worldwide shutdown that lasted nearly eighteen months. All the amazing plans I had in place for the company, building on the successes of 2019, suddenly came to a halt. The list of goals and ideas did not seem possible; customers weren't buying, and plans for the farmers market were canceled. Everything came to a standstill and business was dismal.

The filming stopped for my cooking shows and so did the idea to host in-person cooking classes. This was one of the items on my list to keep moving the company forward. I became frustrated and had reached my boiling point because I had other responsibilities besides running a company. I was the caregiver to my parents and manager of my household while trying to write this book, and now I was distracted by COVID-19.

It was overwhelming trying to manage the fear of COVID-19, the risks of my business temporarily closing, and the ongoing care for my parents. It felt like there was no balance of anything. Being limited in resources and struggling to keep the company going finally took a toll on me. I felt mentally drained and lacked motivation.

I found myself looking for opportunities and could not find them; I quickly realized that I needed to be innovative and create opportunities for myself. I relentlessly researched the internet looking for subject matter on business building and development that would help me to adapt to the changes and better serve my customers.

I also realized that I had the advantage of already being established as an online business. While many storefront businesses had to move in that direction and start from scratch building an e-commerce website, I was ahead of the game; all that I needed to do was evolve the opportunities.

These practices helped me implement new revenue models to increase monetization and stay the course as the pandemic manifested. Some of what I did included collaborating with three women entrepreneurs to create growth for them while expanding my business with their products of local honey, specialty teas, and handcrafted crocheted coasters.

One was already established with her teas. The other two had just started their businesses when COVID-19 struck. With my encouragement, one of them mimicked the way I funded my company and she started a honey business. The other was someone I knew who also had just implemented her artisan crocheting. When I saw their limited opportunities to sell their products, it gave me the idea to collaborate with them. I had the advantage of already running an online business. I did not have to get approval from upper management since I get to make the decisions. Not only did I help these women to keep their businesses relevant, but their products also helped me to expand my products line by adding a gift shop featuring their products.

Rather than dismissing the idea of in-person cooking classes, I took the risk of offering them virtually at a competitive price, which allowed families to be able to eat healthy during a shutdown and to learn the art of cooking. The benefit from this risk turned out to be one of the best decisions. What started out with a few students grew into a well-attended classroom.

Since I had to stop filming the TV cooking show, I pushed myself to learn a new skill that kept the momentum by making my own short cooking clips and posting them to my social media platforms to stay on top of mind. I also realized I was saving money and still getting the message out.

Despite a multitude of setbacks of the COVID-19 pandemic, those circumstances also created opportunities that played a role in the success I am experiencing today. Being homebound with limited business opportunities, I was forced to slow down—

that gave me a fresh perspective on how to thrive. I saw this as an opportunity to work on the new direction I wanted for my company, which was to first prioritize the cooking classes and healthy lifestyle, then my chef services, and finally the bakery. This would still align with my path of wellness, just in a different way.

The pause that came with COVID-19 was a reminder of how quickly something good or bad can change. Having to adjust to different ways of getting things done and finding new experiences has taught me that whenever a crisis strikes, you should pay attention to what's going on. Don't panic. Look for the positive in what is happening. When you pause and observe your surroundings, finding solutions becomes less intense. I adapted to change and survived the pandemic with three attributes.

- **Simplicity:** Initiate an idea with the intent for sustainability, longevity, and simplicity. I removed what wasn't bringing me joy and success. I quit taking on catering orders that were not yielding a profit because I was accommodating the client more than myself.
- **Innovation:** Adapt by changing directions. During the pandemic, I found ways to create products and services that impacted health and wellness that was heightened during this time. When I couldn't host in-person cooking classes, I turned them into online cooking classes. I collaborated with three women business owners to incorporate specialty teas, local honey, and handmade

artisan coasters into my café. I privately labeled a gourmet coffee blend and an amazing all-purpose seasoning consisting of twenty-seven herbs and spices in one jar.

- **Resilience:** Be persistent and resilient in accomplishing your business goals despite challenges; this is key during any unexpected setback. It's not a one-size-fits-all scenario. Do not compare yourself to others, and do not doubt yourself. Just focus on moving your business forward and measure your progress on your own terms.

I believe the key to resiliency is being flexible, persistent, and open-minded. You need resilience to help you adapt, challenge, and recover from whatever the situation is to accomplish your goal. With persistence you will be able to thrive and push through your efforts in the challenging situation. And being open-minded empowers you to see opportunities you may not have considered before.

By staying virtually visible and involved with the community, I was interviewed by an AARP and Federal Reserve Bank of New York research company supporting small businesses to discuss my experiences as a minority woman in business and what changes I would like to see. I took the opportunity to speak on behalf of all women while addressing the stigmas of women who look like me. They found my input highly valuable and returned to shadow my journey as I continue to thrive after COVID-19.

I shared in this interview some myths that have kept women underrepresented as leaders:

- Women are too sensitive.
- Women are fragile and unable to withstand challenges.
- Women cannot match the intelligence of men.
- Women should focus on taking care of the home and family.
- Women are "mompreneurs" rather than business owners or founders.

COVID-19 did not work for a lot of businesses. As the months went by, it worsened, and business opportunities lessened. Despite all my efforts applying for small business loans, grants, and assistance, I kept being denied because I did not qualify for ridiculous reasons. I was back to square one, facing the unfairness of running a woman-owned business with fewer than five employees and being a woman of color with a certain ethnicity. Reasons for not qualifying for business loans or grants included that my business was located online or in an outer lying area and that I didn't have enough overhead expenses to qualify as operation costs because I did not have ten or more employees. Yet I was contributing to the survival of the economy with my company.

I handled my frustrations and denial of assistance by making a budget using the profit margin of 2019 to keep up for as long as I could. I reduced my employees' hours so I could keep them on the payroll, and I didn't pay myself.

Like most places, due to the shutdown, the TV station was not allowing in-person spots or interviews, so my cooking segments were put on hold. After making their own adjustments and everything going virtual, seven months into the shutdown the team reached out to ask if we could try cooking virtually. And we made it happen. Before we went on air, I would have my husband deliver the taste tester for the reporter and anchors to have while the show was being aired. Making significant adjustments were key to keeping my brand and the company pertinent.

By staying the course as resident chef of WBTV-Charlotte through virtual broadcasting, I stayed visible, and that brought new customers and students to the online cooking classes. I adjusted my services by copying the trend of curbside delivery, except I offered contact-free and free Friday deliveries, which a lot of customers appreciated.

Eventually, I took the chance of joining two farmers markets even though I knew I was risking my health, but I needed to survive this pandemic if I wanted to exist. I set aside my fear and ventured out, practicing all the safety measures while focusing on getting the job done.

Despite numerous attempts at staying resilient, the financial impact kept increasing. I was putting in extra hours of baking to entice the farmers market customers—and just when it started to work, some new vendors entered one of the markets and took that opportunity away. Eventually, I ended my relationship with that market because it was not worth my efforts any longer. I was now reduced to one market which was smaller and had less traffic.

Faith and perseverance equal success stories. As 2020 ended and the pandemic worsened, I remained hopeful and determined to grow the company before the year ended because it was one of my goals. I fervently took steps to make this happen.

Recipe for Success:

Being Agile and Resilient

Be open to viewing and
trying things differently.

View challenges as opportunities.

See what is unexpected as a
welcome surprise to learn more.

Make continuous learning an
ongoing aspect of being in business.

Simplify based on what brings
you joy and success.

Pay attention to what is happening
and see how it can be beneficial.

Chapter Sixteen
Spicing Things Up

've experienced success and failure over the years. But by changing my mindset, I survived and pivoted with a 60 percent growth rate during the two years after the pandemic.

Staying innovative is no easy task. I face the challenge of having to adjust constantly to the rapid changes in the industries I'm in. I inspire and stimulate my innovative thinking on an ongoing basis because I love what I do and the journey I'm on. You must first love what you are doing so that the desire to continue daily becomes easy when faced with challenges and obstacles.

Putting this way of thinking to work during the pandemic, I became involved with the smaller farmers market board members and shared ideas to improve and develop the market to increase the volume of customers and vendors; within two months, the market came alive with a larger crowd and more vendors. When customers learned that they could shop for fresh local foods in an open space with social distancing, they showed up every Saturday and most would place preorders, which was a huge success for me.

This action brought new opportunities for my business. Since there was a shortage of businesses that could still operate, and because I was visible at the market, I was sought after for my services. I had the privilege of working with one of the local hospital's cafeteria team providing my chef services and bakery items. I also worked with various corporations and organizations pursuing to improve their employees' and members' health, wellness, and team-building relationships through my online cooking classes.

I succeeded by working with a local coffee roaster to private label my first blend of coffee—*Ren's Stress Less Blend*. I felt the name was quite fitting considering all I'd been through. Customers loved the quality and taste, and coffee sales increased. My pilot season of online cooking classes became a new addition to the company after the attendance increased tremendously. I then decided to turn it into another service to grow my brand, and I developed lesson plans and marketing materials, including class aprons.

As a part of my cookbook and cooking classes expansion, I wanted to create a private label of herbs and spices that are essential to me in everyday cooking and are used in my cookbook recipes. I wanted to offer a blend of high-grade ingredients in one jar so that the customer can save time and money without sacrificing quality. After gathering the information, I started the process; by early summer of 2021, I had privately labeled my blend of herbs and spices in one jar. *LadyRen Chef's Blend* turned out to be a bestseller as customers learned about it. If you can dream it, do it.

You must stay vigilant by adapting to changes in order to build and create new ways to gain revenue. To do that, you must be creative and find ways to outthink your competition. It takes a lot of energy and time to stay focused on finding the best one-of-a-kind ideas. For example, I asked myself this question: "What am I selling?" And it was my answer that drove my innovation: "I am selling experiences and reactions." When customers purchase my products and services, they must have an astounding reaction, one that leaves a memorable experience that makes them come back for more.

Running out of ideas is also another setback, but you must keep pushing through and find new or better ways. I redirected the negative situations into positive ones by stepping back and extracting the positive elements to make it worth my while.

Despite the grueling struggle to survive the pandemic's wrath, 2020 had turned out to be my best year for self-growth and financial success. I owed many of the achievements to my innovative actions. And although it was not easy, it made me more powerful and resilient.

As 2021 progressed, so did I. I returned to the farmers market and had the perfect opportunity to launch my herbs-and-spice blend. I also learned how credibility and authenticity play a major role in a business. My customers never gave up on me. They were eager to have me back because they missed not only the products but also the relationship.

To stay on track, I needed to find new connections while maintaining my current ones. I placed myself in a business organization where I could grow with the right people. Since that time, not only have I strengthened my public speaking skills and participated in a TED Talk style event, but I have also positioned myself for another stream of income by becoming a healthy lifestyle consultant where I share my stories of growing up in a healthy living lifestyle and how to create healthy work habits. I also acquired some contracts for catering services and speaking engagements.

When I had the idea to start my own cooking show, I realized that I didn't have to wait for a television food channel to promote my work. With all the available free social media platforms, I could create my own show. So, I hired a videographer and an editor, and I used my husband's cinematography skills to form my own production team; we began filming cooking segments in my home kitchen as a part of my cookbook marketing strategy.

On New Year's Eve 2021, when I reviewed my goals list, I was pleasantly surprised to see that not only had I achieved all the goals I'd set, but I had also gained additional success with new prospects, despite the multitude of lemons life gave me.

Recipe for Success:

Seeing Positive amid Disaster

You can grow during slow times.
You just need to shift a little.

Stillness brings you clarity
and a stronger direction.

Multiple streams of income
are your life preserver.

Be willing to think outside the box.

Chapter Seventeen
Secret Ingredient Is YOU

The valuable lessons of self-reliance that set the stage for me to survive on my own when I emigrated to the United States at age twenty-one have served me well in being a business owner. It was a new place with people I didn't know, customs I wasn't familiar with, and foods I was unaccustomed to.

I pushed through many dark days working jobs as a babysitter, pet sitter, and housekeeper. I survived by reminding myself that I am in a new place, and I better adapt fast, or I'll be stuck. As the saying goes about New York: "If you can make it there, you can make it anywhere"—there's much truth to that.

While working, I took classes at several colleges to get my foot in the door for better opportunities and stayed current by enhancing my learning with an American education. My parents always believed in the value of lifelong education, so I embraced this even though it was not easy. I college-hopped, paying for a course for one semester or two, gaining the skills and knowledge desired in a certain field, then took a break until I accumulated enough funds to take more courses. I'd test the waters of different colleges to learn new things in different ways. My college-hopping days continued my growth as a well-rounded, open-minded problem solver. Picking up skills and education in several fields has added great value to my business mindset.

Prior to becoming a business owner and celebrity chef, I was an office and recruiting manager and worked in real estate and on Wall Street. But before that I went straight out of college and got on a plane, migrating to another country with dreams of a great career and lavish lifestyle.

When I got married, my husband, who is also from South America, enjoyed continuing our love of the culturally diverse foods we ate growing up. Our home became the place that family and friends visited for holiday celebrations because of my expertise in cooking and knowledge of healthy eating. So when the life-changing challenges struck in our relocation, I relied on those skills to help me with the next phase of my life for a sense of normalcy and a confirmation that not all things have changed for the worse.

I am telling you all of this about my past to make a very important point. Everything you have done and experienced throughout your life is what makes you unlike anyone else and uniquely equipped to do what you are best at doing better than anyone else. Disregarding aspects of your past because you may think it is not relevant to who you are or need to be today is shortchanging yourself.

For years I allowed other people's opinions to influence me, and that was because I was afraid of failure and didn't want to disagree with some of them. I saw failure as something bad and that it would reflect poorly on me.

After all I have experienced over the past ten years specifically, no one can convince me to do the opposite of my intuition; I must be who I am and act on what I now know I bring to the table. Fitting in is not a recipe for success. Being authentically you is your secret weapon in your life and in your business.

Having a vision of where you want to go, understanding your strengths and talents, and harnessing your ability to adapt to change are all going to drive your business forward. Tapping into your skills and being able to use them to overcome any challenge is where your best opportunities lie.

In March 2021, during a TV interview in honor of women's history month, I was asked to explain what made me start my business and what challenges I've experienced being a woman business owner. My answers were not just focused on challenges related to being a woman business owner. For me, speaking on all business fronts was more valuable than being in a victim mindset related to being a woman owning a business. Being true to myself, as I mentioned in chapter 5, also meant being true to my heritage and my cultural background and having a sense of pride in where I came from and what I have been through. Being an innovator meant facing challenges related to being ahead of my time.

Being respected for being innovative was a challenge I shared when I first got started in my business. Many people did not respect the value of my business because it was not a brick-and-mortar store. My books and bakery business were online and no one in my industry was doing this at the time. This certainly changed when COVID-19 hit. I believe my innovative approach finally was recognized as astute and forward-thinking after the pandemic.

That lack of understanding of my business model, potentially in combination with being a woman, contributed to an inability to acquire grants or any other financial support, hindering my growth and making it harder for me to thrive.

Another factor I shared included the lack of diversity. Being of South Asian ethnicity, people prejudged me without getting to know me or understanding the value of my contribution. However, as I stated earlier, I initially tried to hide the aspect of who I was, and this was a big mistake.

All of this is to say that once you realize you are your business's secret ingredient, you can step forward with confidence to leverage this in distinguishing your business. Because of all that you have experienced, your unique talents and skills, and how your journey has brought you to the business you own today, you have wisdom and value unlike anyone else.

There is no perfect plan to run a business because things change each day, but by implementing some strategies that leverage your unique superpowers and experiences, you can prevail. I consider creative thinking and confidence to be most helpful for me to succeed as a business owner, and I believe the same could be applied to you.

Being a creative thinker keeps you open-minded and helps you visualize what your goals would look like if they were a reality now. As you visualize and imagine these goals, you will find ways to creatively solve problems. Then stay focused on moving toward achieving your goals.

If you don't see yourself as creative, let me assure you that you are. Find something simple that you are passionate about, then try to change it in a different way. This behavior sprouts creativity. Pause, reflect, and reevaluate your talents and skills because creativity is ignited in that way by embracing what you do best in creative or different ways.

I want to take a moment to talk about the importance of doing what you say you will do and keeping your word. There is nothing like credibility to either make you or break you. I am a person of my word. If I say I will do something, I follow through. This trait has been my strongest suit and represents my business well. When my name is mentioned, people react with positive remarks. Be authentic; do not pretend to be who you are not. Speak truly about your business, your work, and you. Do not mislead others about your services and experiences, especially in a lifestyle business where you, as the owner, are the face of the business. What you do and don't do reflects upon your business either positively and negatively.

Another aspect of embracing yourself as the business's secret ingredient is in establishing your signature style that is a reflection of what you love, your heritage, your passions, or what makes you and your business unique. The first step to defining your secret ingredient is reconnecting with your tastes. I've seen many businesswomen wearing signature pieces of jewelry, clothing, or outrageous outfits that represent their style. My style is classic. I grew up as a little fashionista following my mom's dress code, so you won't find me wearing a chef's coat or apron when I'm performing for TV cooking shows or public events. People have come to know me for my style and fashion.

I love bright colors and, just like my attire, my website logo is bright and colorful. I believe it draws some attention and adds an ingredient of interest to my business and what I do since people remember me for my style, which led to my blog, *Food, Fashion, Family*.

Believing in myself and having the confidence to take risks and go after opportunities has helped me to be persistent in what I want and overcome obstacles, which has contributed to my success. Once you learn how to stay true to yourself and create an intentional mindset, you will realize that the secret ingredient to your success is you. Plus, the love, support, and encouragement of the people you're surrounded with will strengthen you to be all that you can be. That's when you know you can tackle any challenging recipe that comes your way.

Recipe for Success:

Recognizing Your Uniqueness

All your experiences prepared
you for where you are right now.

Your opinion of yourself
is most important.

Fitting in is not being true to you.

Problem-solving is creative thinking.

Pause, reflect, and reevaluate
your strengths, skills, and talents.

Establish your signature style and own it.

Chapter Eighteen
Recipe Becomes Clearer

learned how strong and resilient I am as I faced what was about to knock me down. While I was planning to kick off 2021 with my amazing list of goals, the universe had other plans in store for me. I had just finished celebrating the holidays with well-deserved time off and was ready to get back to work. Then one morning, unexpectedly, my father passed away. He was a wonderful, loving, amazing, and educated man who added joy to my days with jokes, quotes, or advice. When I was sprinting to the finish line and becoming exhausted, he'd remind me it's a marathon. I always told Dad that he was second place to Mahatma Gandhi. Losing him impacted me at the deepest level.

The days following were even more challenging because we were still in the midst of the pandemic with a lot of restrictions and supply shortages that reduced my production. Added to this was the delay of my kitchen remodel. What was to take three weeks to complete took almost four months. My home was a disaster with boxes stacked everywhere. I couldn't operate the business because there was no workspace. I had no kitchen, which meant having to rely on takeout for meals, and that in turn started to affect my health. For almost four months, there was little revenue coming in to the business, yet I had to maintain the monthly expenses.

I became drained from the stress and constant changes of COVID-19, along with coping with the loss of my father. I took a break and informed my customers and business colleagues that I was temporarily closing the business while I figured out my next steps.

Sometimes a sudden string of awful days and setbacks can actually help us find new perspective. During my sabbatical, I did a lot of reading, self-care, and some business forecasting, which did me a lot of good. Two months later, I returned to work with some plans and ideas that were carefully broken down into steps and methods to take. Most of these involved research and connecting.

For a very long time, I dreaded being asked what I do. I struggled explaining to people about my business because I had several products and services and couldn't figure out the perfect polished way to say it.

One evening I hosted a cooking class that my friends Ed and Kathryn attended; while having dinner, our conversation circled around to being small business owners and how we are viewed by others. I shared how I struggle when asked, "What is it that you do or sell?"

After a lengthy discussion, Ed remarked, "That is because many people in the business world still think that you go into a business to sell widgets, and that's all you do. You keep trying to expand and sell more widgets, bigger and better widgets, but only widgets. You are not selling widgets; you are selling your expertise."

That was enlightening! I tastefully seasoned my definition of what I do after this epiphany by confidently saying, "I am a celebrity chef and healthy lifestyle connoisseur."

As an entrepreneur, it is important to not lose sight of your mission. Stick to your core values and follow your heart. It is easy to fall for the shiny prospects of new opportunities. Pay close attention to how they could positively or negatively impact the growth, longevity, and mission of your company. There will always be great new ideas, products, and social and marketing platforms. If you buy into everything, you'll begin to lose sight of your mission and can invest yourself out of business. I've had some nearly close experiences with this!

I attribute my business growth and customer retention in nonfinancial terms through living and practicing our values. It is important that our customers experience a welcoming atmosphere and feel comfortable with the way their purchases are handled and distributed. My rating of A+ with the Better Business Bureau speaks volumes to the company's credibility. I achieved this by staying true to my mission and my core values. To help you consider what your core values are and how they may drive how you conduct business, I will share with you here some of my core principles.

- **Accountability:** Acknowledging that I am responsible for my actions, I am willing to own the outcomes of the choices, decisions, and the tasks I am responsible for completing. This makes me deliver the best results because I am holding myself accountable to the business. We take responsibility and accountability for all decisions or actions made by our company.

- **Functionality:** Organizing and managing the various activities performed by the business is essential because they all connect to each other for the functionality of the company—for example, income-generating activities, accounting, and the production of final goods or services. If one of the functions is missing or does not work properly, operations cannot run or may be interrupted.

- **Customer Satisfaction:** Understanding and focusing on my customers' needs is demonstrated through them returning to do more business. Customer loyalty won't come easily if you're not focused on pleasing your base.

- **Trust and Honesty:** Being who I am, customers recognize that I am genuine, honest, and truthful, and they want to connect with me. That connection has led to incredible opportunities. It created my brand loyalty and provided the basis of my consumer-brand relationship. By building trust with customers, they recognize the quality of my products and services and the value in what they have invested. When customers find a business they trust, they return, make repeat purchases, and recommend the product or service to others.

- **Value and Quality:** Meeting and exceeding our customers' expectations leads to more referrals, better ROI, and higher opportunities for growth. This cannot happen without a focus on quality and value.

- **Respect:** People are the center of everything we do with our business and community. We respect everyone and we're a diverse and inclusive company that serves diverse customers.

- **Teamwork:** Working as a team enriches our employees' relationships, and it achieves what individuals cannot do on their own. Making group goals first and personal goals second leads to a better outcome for the business.
- **Giving back:** Charitable giving is a defining principle, so we donate 10 percent of our quarterly sales to animal shelters, literacy programs, and community development organizations that focus on reducing homeless population by providing resources for them.

After my sabbatical, the recipe for my business became clearer. I reflected on my mission and core values to make sure everything I was doing was in alignment. I encourage you to do the same in your business. It is both reaffirming and empowering.

Recipe for Success:

Purpose-Driven Business

Have a mission that speaks to the
difference you are making.

Proudly display and celebrate
your core values as a differentiator.

Make charitable giving a part of how
you appreciate being successful in business.

Seek opportunities that will enhance
and promote your mission.

Focus on your customers and the impact you
want to make with your mission.

Sometimes a sudden string of
awful days and setbacks
can actually help us
find new perspective.

Chapter Nineteen
Cake & Eating It Too

The whole idea behind having a lifestyle business is that it allows you to love your life while having a thriving business. It's like having your cake and eating it too, as the saying goes. Is it really possible? Yes, it is! With focus, intention, perseverance, and most important, being true to yourself.

August 12, 2022, commemorated ten years in business. When I started this journey, I had no idea how it would end up. But one thing I was determined to realize was that it must be successful and evolve over ten years. Why ten? I don't know. It was just a number that came to mind when I started the company.

It took me ten years to get to where I wanted to be. I had failed many times trying to find my way with different strategies, different people, and different methods. Now I know failure is the only way to get to success, and in the end, I've fulfilled my dream. I am a successful woman of color, a business owner who has made changes and created opportunities for other women, and I run my life. I get to save animals, help the less fortunate, and help make the planet a better place. How much better can it be?

On any given day, you can find me working on growing the business while solving a myriad of challenges for my retail, concierge, or consulting customers. LadyRen's Bakery & Books, or LadyRen (as most call me), has become a well-known name around the city of Charlotte and nationwide. And although my company has won the attention of the public as well as some prestigious awards, I do not think of my business as just small, but as an innovative think tank spanning the entrepreneurial world with unconventional moves to improve and satisfy healthy lifestyle needs.

Understanding culture, people's feelings, and how to engage in conversations that help customers are part of my core value of customer service. My background and experiences enable me to provide deeply enriched services with the ability to create and offer customer satisfaction.

For some customers, it is helping them to improve their health. This means changing their eating habits and diets to incorporate more nutritious foods along with changes in exercise. By making small changes, they saw improvement and realized positive results.

Some customers need great food but do not like to bake or even have that knowledge. I help them by creating products that help them enjoy a healthy lifestyle. A customer's difficulty in getting the right ingredients and preparing the items with the result they would like to have is a heavy task for many. I eliminate these struggles by providing the finished products and services that allow them to have a harmonious experience, resulting in the most significant impact on customer loyalty.

A customer's daughter is allergic to nuts. She only orders baked goods from me because she trusts that I will make sure there is no cross contamination of any sort. Because of my assurance, her daughter risked testing macarons from me instead of a bakery they do not have a personal relationship with. This customer has thanked me for providing products specifically to her daughter's needs. Ever since, she's remained a loyal customer.

While many businesses use a sales-oriented approach that will maximize their profits rather than focusing on the customer's needs, I build a customer-oriented approach in which, rather than solving the business's needs first, we solve the customers' problems first. This method allows me to retain my customers and build referrals.

Trust customers to do the right thing because you do the right things. I had overlooked putting a business policy in place when I started the business, and when a customer who was also a friend decided to renege on a large order, I was faced with the dilemma of absorbing the loss of income.

One challenge for many entrepreneurs that they may not realize is their sales mindset. Some approach business just looking to make a sale and then move on to the next person. When they set out to gain the customer's business, they say all the right things to gain initial trust. Once the deal is signed, they fail to keep their promise. If you tell your customers you conduct business a certain way, it is important that you follow through. The real question is this: "Are you really interested in your customers and what they need or the problem they need solved?"

Keep your promises. If you say you will do something, make sure you do it. Should there be instances where you are unable to do as promised, take ownership of your mistakes and apologize, then make it right as best as you can. Be loyal to your customers and give them the experience that you promised, and they will be loyal to your business in return.

If you must change the course of your business, be sure to inform your customers. Keep them updated. I've had several experiences where I was the client of some businesses and when they moved on to other careers or changed jobs, they neglected to keep me informed. I would not recommend those businesses or work with those people again. This is not good for your business.

It is important to view your base of customers like a valuable portfolio and treat your portfolio with care. Frequently share useful information before they ask for it. Keep them informed of any upcoming changes with the company that may impact them. Improve your service by asking for their feedback. Listen to them and make any necessary changes.

When friends and family become customers, you are now taking your relationship with them to another level. You want to make sure that your existing relationship with them does not get ruined because of a business transaction. One of the best business practices is to treat them like any other customer. Be open, direct, and honest, and build the same sense of authenticity and transparency as you would in your communications with any of your customers. This was something I had to reinforce with some of my friends and family. Be clear to define expectations and have their requests written down as you would if a traditional customer was ordering from you. Don't assume anything because you think you know them. When you are done taking note of what they want, inform them of the cost and your terms of payment. Clarifying your expectations from each other helps you to know exactly what they want, and it lets them know what the cost is.

Sometimes relatives may request a huge discount and expect us not to charge them as much as we should; because of that, there might be the temptation to give them an inferior product or service. It's best not to charge anything less than what you can comfortably profit from. Don't reduce your quality or standard of service for any reason. Perhaps you can offer a standard "friends and family" discount, so they know what to expect going forward. Always focus on delivering the best possible product or service you can, and do your best to ensure that they are satisfied.

As mentioned at the beginning of this chapter, having a successful lifestyle business is one that is profitable, growing, and allows you to enjoy and love your life. When other business owners ask me how I have achieved this, I am honest that it can be a challenge, and your business can consume you if you allow it. That is why I believe it is more important to focus on growing your business instead of scaling it. Growth that gets out of your control to manage or doesn't consider your capacity will make it impossible to enjoy your life too.

Regular check-ins with myself keep me balanced. It is very easy to get trapped with the continuous desire for more, forgetting to look at how much we've achieved. We keep focusing on having more and more and more. Understandably, we must work hard and be passionate to achieve success, but how much of that success is considered happiness? How much of it brings joy and peace? I was one of those people going after everything that seemed to be an opportunity or something I should be adding to my business because it's working for other entrepreneurs. But I've learned this lesson: many people embellish their successes; if we are not careful, we can get caught up in their stories, and that is exhausting and sucks the joy out of life.

I am an avid reader and enjoy reading topics about astrology, critical thinking, and self-development. I've learned how to become better at attracting peace and joy even in the most challenging situations. Most of us are focused on all the things we have yet to accomplish and are constantly staring at a long to-do list, which can take a toll on our emotional well-being. Sometimes less is best! Pause and reflect on where you were, what you wanted to achieve, how much you've achieved, and be grateful. The best thing you can do is to recognize your progress!

I am happier with having less to add to my to-do list and résumé but having enough to allow the things that bring me happiness. I enjoy having the luxury of travel and living the life I desire. This is the success of a lifestyle business: to work and enjoy life—rather than work tirelessly to conquer more than you need—because that's your definition of success.

Recipe for Success:

Achieving Work–Life Balance

Being super busy is not always a good thing.

Slow down to think clearly;
reflect and recognize your progress.

Focus with intention and perseverance
on how to be true to yourself.

Stop hanging out with people
out of loyalty instead of intention.

People-pleasing gives away your power.

You have the power to choose how
to react and feel in a situation.

Chapter Twenty
A Sour Twist

As the saying goes, "One's best success comes after their greatest disappointment." I found out how losing at something can be a win when I was one of three finalists competing for the Woman Business Owner of the Year award by the National Association of Women Business Owners (NAWBO). I felt that I had all the qualifications and was confident of winning after my interview with the judges. However, on the night of the awards gala, I was not selected as the winner, and I was filled with waves of emotions. I was disappointed with myself and even felt slightly embarrassed that maybe I was not qualified to be in the race against these other businesswomen after all. Perhaps I was not at their level.

As I fixated on all I might have done wrong, I suddenly had a moment where I was able to see all that I did right. Several things flashed through my mind. I realized that I was a winner the moment I signed up to fill out the application and made it to the top three finalists. I also understood that being selected as a nominee for this award among these other successful businesswomen meant that I was recognized as a business owner who could inspire and empower other women business owners to overcome obstacles and achieve their goals.

I also learned that one of the reasons some people cannot see my vision is because they are looking through a pair of binoculars, therefore their vision is short and limited, whereas I am looking through a telescope to see in the distance. I explore lofty ideas that may not go anywhere while reminding myself that failures are not wasted time; they are opportunities for growth.

One of the feedback items I received during the application process was that I needed to change my vision of offering multiple products and instead build my business with only one focus. If I did not have the confidence to stay true to my vision, I might have followed that advice and ended up shutting myself off from many of my passions.

What this experience has taught me is that I am on the right path in my journey, and that following my heart does work. But more importantly, love and passion breed success. I will *not* change who I am or my vision; I do not adhere to the status quo or what is expected. I will not take my eye off the course of my destination. We are living in a time where if you want to thrive and have big goals for your career and your business, you need to constantly develop yourself and learn new skills.

That night I became a winner by losing and here is how. I was pondering the topic for my next chapter of this book, and by losing, the light bulb came on. Losing has allowed me to share how to embrace disappointment and to understand what responsibility means. You simply must find the salvageable qualities in what feels at the time like rotting lemons.

Responsibility means not blaming anyone or anything for your situation, including yourself. As opposed to taking blame, it is crucial to assess the benefits and impediments of the situation and then take action. When you are responsible for your actions, you can then easily pinpoint what you have done well and what could use improvement.

All problems contain the seeds of opportunity, and this awareness allows you to take the moment and transform it into something better. It is about going out there and being the person you want to be without any feelings of being manipulated by anyone else. Do not be someone who feels they must conform to fit in and do what everybody else thinks they should be doing. Being and doing what you know in your heart is right is perhaps the greatest freedom you could have.

Losing the award changed my view on what a winner truly is. I can now share with you that by accepting loss and keeping my spirits high, I can prepare to face my next competition in more enlightened ways. My past experiences have prepared me to handle failure and to understand that if something comes easily, it's rarely valued or appreciated.

I will continue to stay focused on my vision, mission, and tasks at hand and keep my plans in place. I will not allow failure or loss to be a distraction. Instead, I see experiences like this as opportunities to grow to the next level and take the business to its highest potential.

Your ability to take your business to its highest potential may also be when you are at a crossroads where you choose to believe in yourself instead of believing what everyone around you is saying you should do.

Recipe for Success:

A Winning Mindset

You and your business are good investments.

Choices may lead to mistakes. Learning
from them results in even better choices.

A problem is an opportunity in disguise.

Be responsible for your actions.

Pinpoint what you have done well
and what could use improvement.

There are times to trust your intuition, and
times to trust the wisdom of others.

Failure is not bad. If something comes easily,
it's rarely valued or appreciated.

I will *not* change who I am
or my vision;
I do not adhere to the status quo
or what is expected.
I will not take my eye off the course
of my destination.

Chapter Twenty-One
A Lemon a Day

see failure as the icing on a crumbled cookie. Though the cookie fell apart, it can still be fixed and look even better with the icing on top. By discovering how to adapt and learn from whatever comes your way, you come out stronger and even more together than before. Moving into the future and looking back into the past knowing what I now know is why I can share with you how to turn whatever lemon you are facing into something sweet. Instead of feeling as though you've stepped into that snare of the unknown, you can confidently embrace the beauty of what lies ahead.

Experience has taught me that you don't need to have a lot of money to get started or get the help needed. There is a market to suit your budget; you just need to find it. I had the misleading advice from networking speakers that in order to make money, you must spend money. After following such advice, I feel this is not a one-size-fits-all solution. I endured large credit card bills by investing in events and giveaways that I couldn't afford, thinking I would profit from the investment because I had spent money to make money. These hardships forced me to learn that despite a small budget, you can make progress by acting every day to move your business forward if you are intentional and patient.

To be patient with your business development progress, remember to not compare your business to other businesses. Sometimes we believe other people's businesses are so profitable and successful that we end up making expensive decisions. If you must incur debt to build the business, it might be best to take on what's manageable rather than having so much outstanding debt, especially if you cannot afford to bring the balance down. This leads to feelings of frustration, disappointment, and anger. You must constantly find ways to evolve and stay relevant while keeping your spending in check.

Being confident and resilient is a powerful combination for success when you are dealt lemons. If I did not have confidence in myself and know the worth of my business, I would have denied myself the education I gained from joining a business development program. While being interviewed for acceptance into the program, I received discouraging comments from the mentor. He insisted that I had too many products and that I needed to focus on selling only one (here we go again with that remark). I challenged his remark by informing him that this was how I thrived through the pandemic and continued to make progress—and profit. I showed him examples of how many retail stores have expanded in directions other than their original businesses offerings in order to create multiple streams of income.

When starting and building a business, expect challenges. Every day is an opportunity to start and move forward. If you would like to start a business, do not wait for all the steps to line up before you take that first step. It doesn't work that way. Had I listened to the suggestions of some people, I would not be writing this book because I might still be waiting to start, never getting my foot off the starting block.

Take ownership of your dream by being intentional with what you want and what you don't want. If I waited for the right time to start, I would still be waiting, still focusing on having all the funds to cover each expense, still holding off on connecting and committing to marketing projects, still underestimating myself, still being afraid to take risks. Guess what? Each day is the right time to start small, then take steps to grow.

If I had to do this all over again, the one thing I would do differently is to pay close attention to human behaviors. Some people do not represent who they say they are. In retrospect, my approach would be different. As a result, I would expect to save money, time, and energy; I would make better choices, which in turn would bring me more financial gains. Thus, I would be able to leverage and position my company in a much more efficient and effective manner.

I would communicate better with the people I encounter and look for evidence of trends and proven products and services like mine (or close to mine) to verify that those people have the talent or expertise I am looking for to effectively implement the outcome I am seeking.

If I did not experience these unfavorable seasons and thus change my mindset, I would not be as successful as I am now. These experiences caused me to move in different directions rather than quitting or making the same mistakes. So it's all about being intentional, dear reader. *You* must be intentional. You must know your audience. You must know what you want to accomplish. This is what I enforce now and want to be sure

I shared with you, because there might be quite a few women who have experienced the same journey as I have. Maybe you're in a new place. You don't know people; you're starting something new to you. And you're left with the question of "How do I start this business?"

Recipe for Success:

Turning Lemons into Lemon Bars

Anticipate that problems will arise,
and then rise to each challenge.

Be open to options, alternatives,
and thinking differently.

See lemons as an ingredient to
your success, and they will be.

The taste of lemons depends
on how you define the flavor.

Without lemons there
would be no lemon bars.

Each lemon serves a purpose
and brings an experience.

Chapter Twenty-Two
Sweet Lemon Bars

When I first birthed this company, it was just an idea written on a paper napkin while sitting in a coffee shop with my husband, Keith. From then to now I can proudly say that I have many success stories to share while telling the unsuccessful ones.

By being true and believing in myself, I challenged the lemons that life kept tossing at me and I became unstoppable. I turned the lemons into a magical recipe of Super Star Lemon Bars, which took me to the next level of growth and beyond. Once customers got a taste of them, they craved more. I even created a recipe for the gluten-free market.

When I opened my business in August 2012, I had those lemon bars and one children's book, *A Frog in Grandma's Cup*. Since then, I've expanded to over two hundred bakery items and even added options for gluten-free, vegan, and dairy-free customers. I wrote a second children's book, *Mystery Picnic on Stone Mountain*, which was a choice selection of the publisher to be featured at the BookExpo America. I even added a line of freshly made fruit jams that were featured in several consignment stores.

My revenue grew and allowed me to write a third book, except this one was a cookbook, *Just Eat: Pure and Simple Cooking*, which won a Platinum MarCom Award the same year it was published. I have taken my business to a level where I now pick and choose my offerings.

I've created a private-label gourmet coffee blend and a private-label collection of twenty-seven herbs and spices in one jar. I wanted to give customers the opportunity to cook more, eat better, and save money. I became visible in the community and started positioning myself in places for opportunities. By doing so, I built my brand and made a name for myself. I am involved in many community services, including being an advocate of animals and an empowerment speaker to educate and encourage young girls on the importance of education.

To grow the business, I embraced new opportunities: selling at local farmers markets, speaking and volunteering at the Rotary Club, and filming cooking segments for one of Charlotte's TV weekend news (WBTV), which started because of a connection at the farmers market with a news personality, who after tasting my Super Star Lemon Bars declared that I must be on their show. If you recall, I was thrown a lemon when I had to shift to farmers markets versus having an actual storefront. After that one cooking segment, I became a resident TV chef for that show.

Rather than immediately seeking a bank loan that would create an additional expense to our family budget, I used some personal funds and a credit card to get started. This method kept me accountable, and I stayed within my budget. With a bank loan I would have to worry about the high interest rate and if I would make enough sales to cover the minimum balance they require.

Every day I continue to challenge myself and enrich my expertise. During 2021, I was looking ahead and thinking of my next step. I was starting to feel the labor intensiveness of the farmers market preparation, and I needed to cut back on my baking volume without it affecting my customers' needs. I came up with the idea to provide a bimonthly bakery menu, and it worked. This allowed me to still fulfill orders but with a less intense schedule.

The other service I implemented was a concierge chef service which fell under the umbrella of my cooking classes. Since I had already identified my customers' problems and needs for conscious, healthy lifestyles without restrictions, I took the concept of my cooking classes to the next level. I tested the market for my Elite VIP Concierge Chef service where I go to the client and show them that delicious food is more than a meal. I offered a dining experience that starts with a stellar menu of appetizers and entrées and ends with an amazing dessert. Clients are invited to observe how the food is being prepared while learning about the ingredients and health benefits, adding to the personable culinary experience. Unlike the cooking classes, this can be used as an intimate event for the client to enjoy for their personal celebrations or a luxury event among peers to demonstrate elegance and grandeur.

I separated myself from the competition in the crowded market of private chefs and instead focused on a target market need where clients are seeking high-quality experiences with the added value and benefit of authentic, personable, and charismatic service for a fulfilling outcome. The offering attracted new income and, as a result, the bottom line of the business turned a profit by 45 percent. Revenue for that quarter increased while costs and expenses decreased. Clients were eager to be a part of this elite service and willing to pay for the value it brought.

My plan is to slowly move away from the heavy lifting and offer similar services in a different way. From pushing the boundaries of how much I could realistically get done in a certain amount of time to working overtime to cut costs for kitchen rent, these physical and mental demands of the bakery need to shift. Growth has taught me that if the quality of your work is taking a toll on your personal life or health, then your workload may be too heavy. This is how I continue to work smarter, not harder.

I will make my books the appetizer, the chef expertise the main course of the business by breaking it down into categories, and the bakery will become dessert (pun intended) on a smaller scale with a schedule. I have structured my business plan to focus on this shift.

The chef expertise will consist of a category of options including our Elite VIP Concierge Chef provided to a niche market. Cooking classes will be divided into four options: virtual through my website, prerecorded (cooking on demand) and available on a lifestyle media platform, live where viewers tune in, as well as in person when I acquire a kitchen space.

Today, I am a more efficient, confident, and successful woman business owner. I created the framework that changed the way I ran my company by being mostly unconventional in the way I planned, launched, and developed my business. I am an innovator who manages levered cash flow after initially starting with an online gourmet bakery and bookstore; I am one who added concierge and consultant services and an expanded line of bakery products and cooking classes.

Thriving in my mission to enrich people's lives with better-quality foods and education for a healthy, literate, and productive future, I consider myself a healthy lifestyle connoisseur.

I am focusing on taking the business in a different direction by becoming a consultant and speaker on the topic of healthy eating, sharing information on cost benefits and ways of saving time and energy when preparing healthy meals.

Eventually, my objective is to sell the company and to create partnerships with assisted living facilities to help seniors enjoy a quality of life that makes their golden years more fulfilling.

I am focusing on taking my role in a different direction by developing my brand. Now that I've built the company, my objective is to sell LadyRen's Bakery & Books and build the Renate Moore Healthy Lifestyle Connoisseur brand. This will entail two types of products and services.

Products will focus on my cookbook and spice blend with the creation of several Ayurveda blends. Services will focus on keynote speaking with culinary engagement that features a health topic with a baking or cooking activity. This will be offered to banks, organizations, women's groups, corporate businesses, and will be made available for retreats and team-building activities as well as business diversity, equity, and inclusion services and other events.

My chef services will also be a part of the brand. I have secured and acquired the necessary website domain and URL and started formatting the flow chart process of the business growth plan. I am working closely with a business coach on implementing the next steps and have an estimated date for a soft launch in late summer-early fall 2023 around the same time this book is published. These days, life is pretty awesome...

- I get to indulge my passion for travel.
- I continue to invest in myself and my business. I choose who I want to work with and where I want to attend for speaking engagements.
- I have the freedom of controlling my schedule and workload. To work with the ebb and flow of my body, energy, and creativity (and I can take a random trip to the mall if I feel the need).
- Every day I get to inspire passionate people to follow their soul, bravely share their talents with the world, and become the leaders they were meant to be.

I hope that my story inspires and motivates you to be open-minded and fearless in achieving your goals. I am on a quest to create a platform that empowers and inspires more women entrepreneurs to be their authentic selves. My goal is to help you embrace this recipe for entrepreneurial success in your lifestyle business—with a dash of unwavering belief in yourself. If I could leave you with just one thing, it would be this: let go of your fears, doubts, and anxieties, and just take the leap. Every day is the right time with a great formula to *Believe, Focus, Plan, Execute.* And if there's one thing I'm sure of, it's that passion, purpose, and a hefty dose of bravery will get you anywhere.

I summarize all of this not to pat myself on the back but to reinforce to you how unstoppable you can be if I could be, especially when you have perfected the recipe for success in a way that only you can do!

When life gave her lemons, Renate created these Superstar Lemon Bars, which quickly became a fan favorite from her bakery.

About the Author

Celebrity chef and business owner Renate Moore is the founder and CEO of LadyRen's Bakery & Books; her legacy to leave behind is being a fearless achiever and a promoter of girl power!

Renate provides culinary expertise to help people achieve their aspirational healthy lifestyle and connects generations and community through food. She makes it simple to create healthy habits without restrictions so that everyone on all levels can enjoy a wholesome, literate, and fulfilling life. Renate has a passion for providing food that's good for people and for the planet, and she skillfully demonstrates strategies through cookery advice to strengthen family, workplace, and community relationships. She strongly believes that instituting healthy cultures starts at the table and when executed properly, breeds connection, joy, and support.

Renate has over thirty years of success in the kitchen and lifestyle discipline. Maintaining a standard of excellence in healthy lifestyle, leadership, and community service has resulted in awards and recognition, including her Platinum MarCom award-winning cookbook, her role as resident chef at WBTV-Charlotte, her featured profile in KNOW Charlotte's book of fifty influential women (Volume 4, published by the KNOW Women Global Media Company), her receiving the 100 Women to KNOW in America 2023 Award (by the KNOW Women Global Media Company), her nomination for Women for Animal Welfare by the Humane Society of Charlotte, her appearances on several business-enrichment podcasts, and her role as a media spokeswoman.

As a result of her commitment to support women, she promotes female empowerment and influences her environment by sharing her professional skills and the necessary attitude to pass along that empowerment to other women. She accomplishes this through bringing awareness of the circumstances and obstacles that many working women face and through finding ways to eliminate those barriers, inviting other professionals to follow in her example. Those who engage with Renate walk away inspired, encouraged, and confident because of her positive mindset and genuine compassion.

Born and raised in British Guiana, South America, to two ambitious and hardworking parents, her dedication to health and wellness stems from her upbringing, where she and her brother worked alongside their mother in the kitchen helping with meal preparation.

As a young girl she was taught by her parents that she could achieve whatever she set out to do, and as an adult she did that. While living in New York, she achieved successful careers in industries on Wall Street as well as in real estate and international education. Renate is always seeking ways to enhance her skills and has recently become an alumnus of Goldman Sachs 10,000 Small Businesses program.

Renate has written and published three books—two children's books, one of which was featured at the BookExpo America at the Javits Center in New York; and one award-winning cookbook—as well as several recognized articles focusing on entrepreneurship and health and wellness.

Renate's ability to adapt to change is one of her strongest suits, and she is passionate about sharing how to develop that attitude with her peers.

Although Renate's life has grown from calm to storm, as a renowned businesswoman, she appreciates quiet moments with the sounds of nature. When she's not traveling, saving animals, baking, writing, cooking, educating, or engaging with her philanthropy services, you can find her tucked away with a good book or knee-deep in dirt while she gardens.

Recipe for Success:

Girl-Power Legacy

Create through being an example of
equality and success for women and girls.

Be a role model, helping them to live
productive and fulfilling lives.

Teach them to be confident to make decisions
and achieve things independently.

Help them know they have the
strength to reach their full potential.

By recognizing their skills and talents,
they can be unstoppable like you.

Acknowledgments

Having an idea and turning it into a book is as hard as it sounds. The experience is both internally challenging and rewarding. Writing about the story of your life-changing journey is a surreal process. None of this would have been possible without my awesome publication team who helped me so much. It is because of their efforts and encouragement that I found the will to share my story. SPARK Publications, with special thanks to Fabi Preslar, my ever supportive and patient publishing manager; Sherré DeMao, my amazing editor, for her editorial help, keen insight, and ongoing support in bringing my stories to life and for getting the manuscript done before the due date.

A very special thanks to Mrs. Velma Jackson. She was the first friend I made while standing at the bus stop when I moved to North Carolina. Her warm welcome and love helped me with the process of getting acclimated.

Thank you to Coach Babette, the business coach, for teaching me the difference between a schedule and a to-do list, and what a good business coach represents.

To my family. To my incredible husband, Keith, for always being the person I could turn to during those dark and desperate years. He sustained me in ways that I never knew that I needed. To my son, Keith Jr., for the reminder when I was at the brink of giving up that "we have to acknowledge our failures. Even if we don't succeed, we still use them to help push ourselves forward." To my daughter Kellieann, for the encouragement by sharing stories of her boy band groups that had many struggles before making it. To my mom, Sheila, for thinking the world of me and seeing my efforts as huge success, and for always telling me how proud she is of what I do. To my dad, George, for the frequent reminder to slow down and not overdo it. Dad passed away before I could finish this book, but he would be happy to know that I've heeded his advice. And to my brother, Fenton, for always supporting me and being a constant in my life, and for the wonderful sibling relationship we have.

To my friends—Kathryn and Edward Isaacs, Kathleen Wilson, Erika Paolo, Mary Erkson, Saila, L, my NC bestie Janel (RIP), Carrie Maxick—for always checking in on me, cheering me on, and seeing me through my good and bad times, my struggles and successes; and for understanding when I couldn't have social time with them. That is true friendship.

I want to thank *everyone* who ever said anything positive to me or taught me something. I heard it all, and it meant something.

Finally, to all those who have been a part of my getting here. Thank you for playing a role in this journey. Thank you for the disappointments and setbacks. Thank you for the love and support.

I want to thank *everyone* who
ever said anything positive to me
or taught me something.
I heard it all,
and it meant something.

Contact Renate

🖥 **www.renatemoore.com**

✉ **info@renatemoore.com**

📷 **@renatemoore**

in **linkedin.com/in/renate-moore**

Printed in the USA
CPSIA information can be obtained
at www.ICGtesting.com
JSHW010829020923
47462JS00005B/19